Life... With No Breaks

Nick Spalding tried to write a book in 24 hours. Turns out that's impossible... it took 30!

Life... With No Breaks is a unique, hilarious and heartfelt look at the modern world we live in, told by a master story-teller with much to say - and only a weekend to say it in.

You'll laugh out loud reading Nick's odyssey of non-stop writing in a collection of anecdotes, asides and stories - all dredged up from an over-stimulated brain functioning on caffeine, nicotine and the occasional chocolate biscuit.

The book is a conversation with you, and with Nick you'll venture into the thorny topics of love, life, sex, horribly timed bowel movements and a deathly fear of sponges (among many other things).

After you've read Life... With No Breaks, you may never look at the world the same way again!

By Nick Spalding

Coronet Books

Love... From Both Sides
Love... And Sleepless Nights

Racket Publishing

Life... With No Breaks
Life... On A High
The Cornerstone

Life... With No Breaks
Nick Spalding

Racket Publishing

Author's Note

Life... With No Breaks was the first book I self-published, way back in the dim and distant days of April 2010, when dinosaurs ruled the earth. The book industry - and my place in it - is a vastly different kettle of badgers now to what it was back then, thanks to the self-publishing phenomenon that started on the Amazon Kindle and proliferated to all eBook platforms faster than you can say 'seventy percent royalty rate'.

I'm one of the very lucky writers who benefitted greatly from this phenomenon - selling a boatload of comedy eBooks that I published on my own, which in turn led to a three book deal with a major publisher.

Chances are you're coming to this book after reading Love... From Both Sides and its sequels. If so, welcome to where it all started.

This book was an experiment.

One that turned out pretty well all things considered, and set me off on the road to where I am now. It's an odd little read I'll cheerfully admit - quite rough around the edges because it's the first thing I wrote, and full of stories more fabricated and embellished than a politician's expenses claim, but if you enjoy my style of comedy (and I'm assuming you do, as you're reading this) then you should have a jolly good time with it.

Try not to laugh out loud if you're in public. The men in white coats will be sniffing around you in no time at all.

Best wishes,

Nick

Chapters

Getting started.

Some would tell you it's the hardest part of writing a book.

They're wrong, though. Starting is a piece of cake. Keeping it going is the difficult bit.

Like having sex when you're over seventy, I'd imagine.

I have no clue how the idea for a book like this came to me. It's not something I'd planned to do. It just popped into my head this morning while I lay in bed.

I had a massive erection as well, but I'm pretty sure the two weren't connected.

Inspiration is a funny thing. There you are, merrily stumbling your way through the day, thinking about nothing more important than fixing the damn guttering before the weather caves in - when *bam*! ...inspiration hits you between the eyes, sending you into a whirlwind of creativity.

The urge to write is something I've been short on of late and my fledgling career as a professional writer - one good enough to make a few quid and sound interesting at dinner parties - has stalled somewhat.

I thought I faced the legendary writer's block, which involves much bemoaning of lots and imbibing of intoxicating spirits.

Happily, I avoided all of this when I woke up thinking:

What if I just sat at the computer and started to write, without a plot or story and no idea where the thing was going? How would it turn out? What would I write? And most importantly... would I end up regretting it?

What you're about to read is the result.

I'm sat at my desk in the study upstairs, the laptop open in front of me - it's a Dell Inspiron 1525 dual core processor with 2gb of RAM, if you're interested in that kind of detail... and if you are, please try to get out more, the sun will do you good. I'm in a fairly comfortable office chair that makes a mournful sighing noise when you lower it and the heating is on because it's been chilly today and I don't want to get blue toes.

A large flask of coffee stands beside me and I will continue to drink from it even when the contents inside get cold and bitter. I also have various snacks to keep my stomach from rumbling - none of them the low-fat variety, which isn't going to help the spare tyre one bit - and the fridge is full, so I can raid it when I need to.

A row of new cigarette packets - replete with enormous health warnings - stand to attention like soldiers, waiting to mount another assault on my delicate lung tissue. They're accompanied by an ashtray stolen from the local watering hole, big enough to contain all the butts I'll crush into it as I try to massage the brain cells into creating a coherent narrative.

Here I am, at nine minutes past six on a drizzly Saturday evening, with every intention of writing a book in one sitting.

No breaks, no brainstorming sessions to sketch out the next plot development on The Simpsons notepad I've got on the desk, and no time set aside to sit back and digest the quality of my prose.

Just me, my keyboard and good intentions.

It's seat of the pants stuff, I can tell you.

I will not stop until I am done!

Unless there's a power cut.

I may have to get up every once in a while to get rid of the coffee in the little boy's room, but you'll forgive me that won't you?

I haven't a clue how long I'll last... no concept of how long my brain and fingers can keep up the pace without going on strike due to physical fatigue or mental breakdown.

Ten pages?

A hundred?

A thousand?

How many hours can I sit here with my arse gradually numbing and the ashtray forming a small mountain of cancerous by-product?

Two?

Twenty?

A hundred?

I'm hoping to get to a decent length for a book.

The kind that's long enough to get your teeth into, but isn't a daunting read. I'll leave the doorstops to the Stephen Kings and Tom Clancys of this world. They're far better at it than I could ever be.

As for subject matter, that's as unknown to me now as I sit here typing, as it is to you at some point in the future, reading the book.

I can see you in my mind's eye...

There you are… a few weeks, months or years down the road, maybe in your favourite armchair with the dog dribbling gently onto the new cushions… or in bed with your partner snoring gently beside you as the rain patters off the window, making you glad you're at home in the warm.

You might be asking yourself:
Where the hell is he going with this?
And perhaps more importantly:
Will there be a point? Will it have purpose? In short… have I just wasted my hard earned money on a book I could have bought some chocolate with?

And there's got to be a point to a book hasn't there? Even one written totally off the cuff like this is.

As I sit here tapping away on the keyboard, I've decided to make it a conversation with *you*, the person kind enough to download Life…With No Breaks and dedicate their valuable time to reading the thing.

It'll be a one-sided conversation admittedly - with me doing all the talking and you occasionally nodding, smiling and agreeing with me when my views happen to coincide with your own.

If you're in public, try not to nod or smile too much, unless you like having a personal exclusion zone of ten metres around you and being thought of as 'the weird one standing on platform two'.

I want us to be friends, of a sort.

Call it a secret friendship, caught in the pages of this book. The kind you don't tell people about for fear of sounding a little strange.

A friendship across time if you will, with me sitting here in a slightly threadbare grey t-shirt, a Marlboro Light hanging from my mouth - and you, wherever you may be, blocking out the world around you in that magical bubble we create when we've got our noses in a good book.

To make this process easier, you can imagine you're here with me if you like - if that's not too weird a proposition.

I've got another chair in the room. It's also quite comfortable, but a little harder than the one I'm in.

Sorry about that: writer's prerogative.

Feel free to take a snack. The cookies are particularly good.

I hope you like lukewarm coffee with one sugar, because that's all I can offer.

If the smoking bothers you, feel free to crack a window.

I've got a menu for the kebab place down the road. They do deliveries, but I tend not to order from there much these days, ever since the guy over-charged me a quid for a chicken kebab with extra cholesterol.

Of course, I don't mind at all if our relationship is dependent on your schedule. No doubt you have important things to do, important places to go and important people to meet. I'm quite happy to sit here and wait for you to come back when you're ready to continue.

That makes me the ideal friend, I reckon...

I'm patient, understanding and won't ignore you for weeks if I think you're having too much fun without me.

I won't borrow money, or return a DVD covered in peanut butter and dog hair that I borrowed six months ago for 'just a couple of weeks, mate!'

I can't buy you a drink in the bar, or give you a lift to work when the car breaks down, but I think the advantages outweigh the disadvantages for the most part.

Sit yourself back then and prepare for the roller-coaster ride that is my life.

We're going to have fun, you and I... and talk the night away.

I'm putting in these time checks so I can keep track of how events proceed, and to create a few chapter breaks that'll stop me rambling.

You'll have to watch me, though.

If I do start waffling, poke me with the broken umbrella behind you.

Let's get to know each other better then.

As there's no way of me knowing your name, I'll make one up. After all, you're acting as my muse for this - and I need a name to put to my muse, don't I?

I'll keep it to myself if you don't mind. It's more fun that way.

You know my name of course. It's there on the front of the book.

Nick Spalding - like the tennis racquet.

Call me Nick, Nicholas or Nicky.

Just not *Nickle-Pickle* like my mother did until I was twelve. I hated it.

Perhaps a good way to start is telling you a bit about me:

I'm a man approaching his forties with the kind of dread usually reserved for prisoners on their way to the gallows. I'm constantly eyeing up the price of Grecian 2000 and nose hair-clippers.

The word *prostate* has taken on new and dark significance in my head and I have the doctor on speed dial, just in case.

You already know I'm a writer, but it might interest you to know I travel quite a lot because of it.

I went to New York for the first time recently, where I saw the memorial where the Twin Towers used to be and had a little cry to myself.

I live in the south of England, where the weather isn't quite as bad, but the mortgage prices are high enough to give you a nose bleed.

We *still* complain about how bad the weather is, of course - we're British, after all - though it hardly ever gets cold enough to freeze water in car radiators or unfortunate dogs to metal lamp-posts.

I watch an average amount of television, turning the sound down when the ads come on.

I've been married. It didn't really agree with me much.

It didn't agree with her either, but we managed to produce a healthy son between us, so things ran smoothly enough to accomplish that at least.

I don't vote and still listen to music I should be ten years too old to enjoy.

I ignore health warnings about the food I eat and try to ignore the ones on cigarette packets.

I'm afraid of needles.

And for some reason - sponges.

I'm not a particularly sentimental man and never enjoy romantic comedies.

I spend too much time worrying about things that are beyond my control, but try not to let it depress me too much.

I once dressed up as a woman for a fancy dress party and thought the knickers felt quite comfortable.

That's enough for now, I think.

All a bit random I admit, but enough for you to get a rough idea of what your new buddy Nick is like.

Nothing too bad in there, eh?

I don't come across as a lunatic, as far as I can tell.

You're going to learn a lot more about me as we go on, but that gives you a flavour... even if it is just vanilla.

We'll add the tasty chocolate sprinkles as we go.

Hey! Look at that.

An hour of writing done and that's the introductions over with.

I'm hoping the time checks won't be quite this frequent through the whole book, as it'll mean the chapters are very short and Life... With No Breaks will be more novella than novel. I'll have to fall back on some of the rude limericks I've heard in the past, just to pad the damn thing out.

Call that first bit the prologue, if you like.

Now it's done and your appetite has been whetted, we'd better get to the good stuff quickly, before your interest wanes and that Discovery documentary you've got running on mute in the corner of the room starts to divert your attention away from our burgeoning relationship.

There's nothing worse than reading a book and having your mind wander.

Sign of a bad writer... and a worse book.

So let's keep your mind focused on me and ignoring what new facts Discovery have unearthed about Hitler.

...actually, I love a bit of Discovery Channel.

I'll watch almost anything they screen if I'm in the mood.

I find the shark documentaries particularly fun to watch, even if it's just for the gory bits.

Don't you think that's the reason why we watch shows like that, when you get right down to it?

We may pretend to ourselves - and others - that we're fascinated with the mating rituals of Basking sharks, but we're actually hoping for grainy amateur footage of some poor bastard being mauled by an irate twenty footer... basking or otherwise.

It's in all of us to one degree or another: the desire to see something awful - or at least strange and unexpected - happen to other people, played out in front of our eyes from behind that safest of barriers: the television screen.

You only have to look at the popularity of reality shows like Survivor and I'm A Celebrity, Get Me Out Of Here, to see that as far as humans are concerned, there's nothing like witnessing other people's misfortunes - and being glad *we're not them.*

It's great fun watching some has-been actor eating a wriggling cockroach, or looking on as a glamour model with the brains of an ice cube is forced into a metal box full of scorpions. It really gets the juices flowing.

And what about the Oprah Winfreys and Jerry Springers of this world?

Those shows are all about watching people air their dirty laundry in public.

We lap it up!

There's nothing like spying into somebody else's life for a good night's entertainment. Especially if they're cocking things up left right and centre – and paying the price for their blunders in a highly amusing fashion.

Extending that thought, what we're engaging in here is along the same lines.

You're reading a book written by a complete stranger, in a single session, all of it unscripted, unedited and - hopefully - honest.

Oh, I may check for spelling mistakes and narrative balls-ups when I'm done, but other than that, it's straight from my keyboard into your brain.

By now - some nine pages and ninety minutes in - I'm hoping I've *grabbed* you.

With any luck you've got a definite interest in finding out what happens next and you'll hang out with me for a while, reading whatever comes spilling out of my head.

I want you to keep reading, and if that means delving into my murky past, then so be it!

Let's see then. Shall we start with a nice embarrassing episode in the life of Spalding?

Something to set us on with a laugh and a smile?

There are quite a few to choose from…

I know. How about this:

I'm twenty two years old, at university and haven't a care in the world.

My grades are good, my friends don't call me Nickle Pickle behind my back and my bank balance is only slightly in the red.

I live in a pokey one bedroom apartment, wash my clothes when I remember to and eat nothing but beans on toast.

I'm never up early enough to hear the postman, but sometimes I'm out late enough to see him as I stumble home.

The horror of things like mortgages, taxes and interest free loans are but distant ships on the horizon of life.

Probably the most important decision in my life right now is whether to drink beer or spirits.

Naturally, I'm loving every minute of it.

I'm in that wonderful period between being a kid and a real adult, where I run my life the way I want - largely at the expense of the British government. This was a time when they still thought it probably wasn't a good idea to saddle the workers of tomorrow with more debt than a small African country.

What I really want right now is the blonde I keep seeing in the student bar every weekend.

She normally stands near the pool table - the one with the unidentifiable stain on it that bares a striking resemblance to Abraham Lincoln - holding half a lager and chatting with her friends.

Her name is Callie.

I have no idea what this is short for, but it sounds enchanting to my ears regardless. I think she looks a little bit like Grace Kelly. But with bigger tits.

I have very little information about her, except she's a year above me on the same degree course. I've also been informed by a friend that she once did a striptease in the student common room at Christmas, but as this friend also maintains his brother - who works in a fish and chip shop - once felt up Naomi Campbell at a cocktail party in London, I'm taking this information with a gigantic pinch of salt.

Not being much of a ladies man, it's taken me several weeks to even think about plucking up the courage to speak to Callie.

And here she is.

At the same party as me.

Gods be praised and we all sing hallelujah!

This makes things much easier. The daunting environment of the student bar has been replaced by the comfortable atmosphere of my friend Steve's house... well, he's more a nodding acquaintance than a friend - it's one of those friend of a friend invites we all know and love.

Parties lend themselves more to relaxed conversation and I'm pretty sure I can spark one up with Callie without sounding like a hormonal sixteen year old.

It's the perfect opportunity.

The stage is set and the show must go on.

Sadly, I'm drunk.

Very, *very* drunk.

I've been drinking since roughly three o'clock that afternoon, in the time honoured tradition of loafing under-graduates everywhere and it's deep into evening by the time I realise Callie the Wonder Girl is in my general vicinity.

But never mind. Alcohol instils confidence!

It should be absolutely *no* problem to venture up to the young lady and charm the pants off her.

I have no doubt that sex of an epic nature is not too far off in the grand scheme of things - providing I can get past that annoying introductory phase we have to negotiate before carnal gymnastics can ensue.

Some back story before we continue, I think:

I was not at this time what you could call *sexually experienced*. My career as a lover amounted to two women and my right hand.

Neither was I experienced in the ways of alcohol consumption - something that would prove an important factor in the scene about to unfold.

An experienced drinker can be very drunk, but still have the where-with-all to hide his level of intoxication and perform as a functioning adult.

I wasn't experienced and therefore had *no* chance.

At about ten o' clock I realise Callie is at the party and what's more, she doesn't appear to be accompanied by a boyfriend.

There's a few guys gathered around her, like bees around the proverbial honey pot, but the alcohol is assuring me they'll be swept away once Spalding The Great enters the fray.

Bearing this in mind, I've worked out an opening gambit:

'Hi. It's Callie, right? You're in the third year of my course. Can you give me a heads up what we're doing next semester?'

Brilliant, eh?

Cool, easy-going and smooth.

Also shows a dedication to my studies, which makes me look like an intelligent guy. One who will help her produce strong and charismatic offspring.

Sadly, I never get the chance to use it.

Concentration is not one of the inexperienced drinking man's strong points, especially when he's passed the ten-pint mark.

Every time I think about using my wonderful ice breaker, my attention is diverted away like a magpie seeing something shiny at the side of the road. It's either the promise of more alcohol, or a favourite song on the stereo that takes me away from the girl of my dreams.

Time slips by.

Ten o'clock rapidly sinks into eleven… and crawls towards midnight.

I'm not drunk by this time.

Oh, no, no, no.

I am *shitfaced*.

Referring back to what I said about alcoholic experience and control over oneself, I didn't just mean control over the mind and emotions - I meant control over the body as well.

After ten pints, the section of your brain that spends its days making sure your bodily functions operate efficiently has buggered off for a nice soothing head massage, leaving you to fend for yourself.

The drunken man isn't good at fighting the effect alcohol has on his complicated organic processes and tends to surrender quicker than a Frenchman in 1940.

Unpleasant things happen next.

I see the expression you're making now. You know what's coming, right? You think you've got things figured out!

You're thinking your new pal Nick strolled up and was sick all over poor old Callie, aren't you?

If only.

I didn't vomit over her. It was much worse than that.

While I'm in the kitchen telling a bad joke - her only a few feet away in the lounge and oblivious to my planned seduction - I slip drunkenly on a patch of beer-soaked linoleum, head butting a kitchen cabinet. My knees buckle from under me, my arse hits the ground hard… and my bowels loosen to the point of no return.

In short - and to put no finer point on it - I shit myself.

My arse hits the floor and the shock makes my teeth rattle. I feel an unpleasant pancake of warmth spreading across my buttocks and the odour of defeat rises from my nether regions.

Even in my drunken state, I know this isn't going to end well.

The first person to react is my mate Sam, who's standing next to me. His cry of disgust is followed by a very loud exclamation that didn't help my humiliation one bit:

'Bloody hell! Spalding's crapped his pants!'

Yes indeed, Spalding *had* crapped his pants.

Something that hadn't happened to Spalding since about the age of two.

Spalding also had a nice bleeding scalp from the head-to-cabinet interface, but that paled into insignificance alongside the whole defecating in public side of things.

Rapidly, those in attendance notice what has befallen me and are starting to arrive at their own conclusions based on Sam's announcement and my location on the floor.

I sit there for a few seconds, letting my inebriated brain digest recent events and trying to sort out an exit strategy from the party.

All thoughts of wooing Callie have flown.

A method of painless suicide is formulating, to avoid the endless embarrassment this night would otherwise cause. I'm nothing if not a forward thinker.

I rise gingerly to my feet, my left hand grasping my backside in a vain effort to prevent the contents of my underwear slipping down my leg.

As my face turns red and my head swims like a pro on steroids, I shuffle past the aghast party-goers and into the lounge beyond.

Yep, there she is. Callie the Wonder Girl - hand over her mouth in horror and eyes as wide as dinner plates.

I offer her a grin.

I don't know what I'm hoping to accomplish with this but it's worth a shot.

I guess I'm trying to convey my feelings about the whole situation in that smile:

'Hey, never mind, eh? These things happen. We'll look back and laugh about it in ten years when we're married and have three kids.'

Except these things didn't just happen... at least not to twenty-two year old undergraduates.

She knows it - I could tell by the way she was backing away from me - and I know it.

...time to beat a hasty retreat.

I do so - not with the sound of ringing laughter, but with a horrified silence only broken by the loud stereo.

As I recall, the song playing was *Help* by The Beatles.

Fitting.

It takes me a few moments to get to the front door. I know as I scrabble for purchase on the lock with one hand - buttocks clasped in the other - that there's a hoard of students looking down the hallway at me, wondering if the entertainment is ever going to end.

I wrench the front door open and shamble off into the night, running like a sailor with rickets.

Thankfully, I only live a couple of streets away.

It occurs to me that I should probably stop and remove my soiled clothing, but I decide not to, opting for a crap covered arse rather than a night in the cells for indecent exposure.

On most nights, there would be virtually no-one on the streets to see me. Tonight though, it seems the world and his wife have decided on a nice moonlit stroll and I have to swerve around several people before arriving back at the flat.

God knows what they made of this partially blood-soaked maniac, running in a bow-legged jog, clutching his rear-end like he's scared it's going to explode. I seem to remember mumbling swift apologies by way of explanation, as if they'd known what had happened.

When something truly awful happens to you, it's funny how you believe the rest of the world cares.

In my mind, there are headlines forming for tomorrow's papers:

PARTY POO-PER SPALDING IN PANT-FILLING PRATFALL!
Pictures on pages 7, 8, 9 & 11!!

I arrive at my flat and run straight upstairs to the bathroom to clean off. This takes quite a while as I'm still as drunk as a skunk.

When the cleaning is over - including some rather painful prodding at the cut on my head with a TCP soaked jay cloth - and I've changed into a pair of clean jogging pants, I sit back on the toilet, stare into space and wonder what the hell to do.

I'm sitting there pondering the possibilities of emigrating to a country thousands of miles away - where no-one speaks English and alcohol is illegal - when my stomach decides it wants in on the action and decides to throw up what hadn't already come out the other end.

Thankfully, no-one's around to see *this*.

In the next few days and weeks, word got round about my exploits.

I couldn't walk through the university campus without thinking people were staring at me and then going to tell their friends that they'd just spotted 'Follow Through Spalding' walking past the library.

I felt it the better part of discretion to avoid social gatherings for a while.

I was expecting lots of barbed witticisms from my friends, but was surprised to find that none of them wanted to mention it.

This was somehow *worse*.

I saw Callie a few times after that night, but tended to drop my eyes and shuffle into the shadows before she had a chance to see me.

I'd like to think I can recover my dignity in most situations, but recovering any from this episode would make raising the Titanic look as easy as boiling a small kettle.

I tended to stick to four pints or less from then on.

…and still do.

Not the most cerebral of stories to kick us off, but I hope it made you laugh.

It might have disgusted you a bit too, but I'm sure I saw a smile spread across your face and heard a small chuckle - which goes to show toilet humour is never a bad thing in moderation.

Let's hope there's no-one with you, because they'll be curious as to why your smiling. Explaining it's because you've just read a story about a fully grown man crapping his pants in public might be a little hard to accomplish and still sound like a mature human being.

There's nothing like a man's humiliating downfall to get the ball rolling, I say.

Please stop looking at my backside like that though - as if something horrendous is about to happen. I'm stone cold sober at the moment and my sphincter is behaving itself. I don't expect it to start playing up again until I'm eighty.

Worry not, I'm sure I can plumb the depths of my memory and recall more embarrassing episodes to delight you with as the book goes on.

There are more than enough to choose from. Though I can't think of any offhand that equal that one for sheer humiliation in the presence of the opposite sex. It amazes me I haven't spent the last fifteen years in therapy.

I can look back on it now and laugh at the whole thing. The passage of time lends a certain objectivity and the humiliation has faded to nothing in the intervening fifteen years.

Almost, anyway.

I don't think it matters how old you are or how wise you get in later life, incidents of extreme embarrassment always retain a degree of shame, no matter what station you achieve in life.

If Albert Einstein had suffered a similar fate, all the Nobel prizes and universally accepted theories of relativity wouldn't entirely put to rest the shame of soiling oneself in public.

Of course, the flip side is we remember the great moments as well.

All the major events in our lives - good or bad - stay with us, while the rest of the garden variety stuff gets washed down the memory drain.

I think you're more likely recall the bad moments however. It's just the way the mind works:

You may have climbed a mountain wearing only a thong...

You may have cured Beriberi disease with nothing more than a spatula, Petri dish and good intentions...

You may have saved twenty bawling children from certain death in a cable car accident...

You may have done all these things, but I bet the memories that jump from your subconscious more often than not are the ones you wish you could forget:

Got caught masturbating by your mother when you were thirteen? *Bang*! It's in your head as your new lover's hand slides down to your crotch.

Thrown in the cells for a night after stealing ten traffic cones when you were eighteen? *Wallop*! There it is as the boss at your new dream job tells you they have to run a background check before you can start.

Had a haircut done by your best friend that made you look like an escapee from the local home for the mentally distressed? *Boom*! There it is as you sit down in *Coiffure Jacques* for that hundred pound cut you've been saving up for over the last six weeks.

Been dancing away merrily to Rihanna in a nightclub, blissfully unaware your skirt has slid down your legs and that all the girls from work are pointing and laughing? *Whack*! There it is as you take to the dance floor for a ceremonial twirl at the wedding reception with your new husband.

We all have them tucked at the back of our minds, in a special locker marked *World, Swallow Me Up* - ready to pop up at a moment's notice and when you least suspect it.

I think this explains why we find solace in the trials and tribulations of others.

Misery loves company after all and there's nothing like sharing your woes and past cock-ups with someone else to make you feel better.

Perhaps that's what I'm doing with my little project here, if I can get philosophical about it for a moment. I'm writing some kind of half-arsed confessional to you, my brand new friend.

I'm not much of a philosopher usually.

It's probably better to let most stuff just wash over you, picking out the bits from the flotsam and jetsam that look important. Over-thinking things leads to tension headaches and an ulcer.

Everyone has to prioritise the important from the trivial. To decide what's likely to have a big impact on your life from what won't.

...the tree coming towards you at forty miles an hour for instance - that's probably quite important.

It'd be lovely to hear about something *you'd* like to forget. I'm as happy to listen to other people's anecdotes as I am recounting tales of my own.

Can't do that with you, can I?

Strictly one-way traffic in this conversation, I'm afraid.

I'm the writer and you're the reader.

How about this then: as you can't tell me, why not grab the nearest person you know and reveal something you'd have otherwise kept to yourself?

Go on, give it a go. It's very liberating, I assure you.

It doesn't matter if it's not as gigantically horrible as my incident at the party.

Maybe you recently farted at an inopportune moment, or blurted out something you probably shouldn't have.

I did that once.

I called a senior female work colleague of mine *mum* during a meeting.

We're not talking the levels of embarrassment I achieved with my little accident, but it certainly made my face red. Hers too, for that matter.

Off you go, then.

Go confess a minor sin or indiscretion to a loved one. I'll sit here and wait for you to come back.

...

...

Back?

Feel better?

Excellent.

Sit back in the spare chair - I've added a nice soft cushion.

The cookies are starting to run a bit low now - who's a greedy little sod, then? - but I've got some microwave popcorn, if you fancy.

I haven't opened the Pringles yet, so you can have the satisfaction of hearing that little *floomp* noise the tube makes when you rip off the seal.

Ok, back to the plot - or lack of it in this case.

What shall we chat about now, as the clock ticks its way past nine o'clock?

Time.

Let's talk about time.

It's a fantastic subject, especially as it plays such an important part in this great undertaking we are in.

People say money rules the world, or love makes it go round, but I reckon what governs our lives more than anything else is that blasted ticking sound that marks off the minutes and seconds.

The clock is up there on the wall, working its malevolent magic. Putting time in a cage and locking you in there with it.

I'm a clock watcher.

One of those people who tends to look at his watch at least two or three times an hour to check how long I've got to a) keep working b) sit on this plane c) wait in this queue d) watch this terrible romantic comedy.

And I'm a stickler for having the right time on that watch as well.

There's nothing worse than it running slow or fast. It cocks up my equilibrium completely.

There are people - I'm sure you know them - who say things like:

'I always have my alarm clock running fast so I've got a bit of extra time in the morning!'

Utter bastards.

If you're so insistent on having extra time in the morning, why not just set your alarm *earlier*?

Invariably, these people are always late for everything anyway - which just goes to show, doesn't it?

Our lives are beholden to the clock on the wall as it ticks off the seconds, minutes and hours.

We wake up to it, sleep to it, work to it and eat to it.

Hell, some of the time we even have sex or go to the toilet to it.

Most of the stress caused in the twenty first century is down to that horrible clock:

If you're at work and have a deadline to meet.

If you're going on a first date and have to be at that small, intimate bistro on the high street at seven thirty.

If you're waiting in line to get a new tyre, knowing your lunch break has twenty minutes left and the queue in front looks like a forty minute wait.

You're a complete slave to the clock and the ulcer it's forming in your stomach lining.

But not to worry!

You'll eventually reach a point where the clock ceases to have a huge impact on your life.

It's called retirement.

No longer will your days be controlled by Seiko, Timex or Tag Heuer.

You'll still have lots to do with any luck - even if it's only a shuffleboard tournament and a spot of light reminiscing - but it'll be according to your own schedule.

It's been said before but I'll say it again:

How deeply ironic is it that the present given to people retiring from fifty years of work is usually a gold clock? At the time of life when the last thing you want to do is ever look at one of the bastards again.

Time flies when you're having fun.

Why?

You're not looking at the bloody clock all the time, that's why!

You've got something occupying you that you're actually enjoying - putting the clock completely out of your head. And when you're not looking at it, the sneaky git goes round at break-neck speed, with no consideration for your feelings at all.

Three hours pass in what feels like three minutes...

On the opposite side of the fence, when you're bored out of your tiny mind and would like nothing more than to spread your wings and fly away, the clock gets slower and slower. This is because you *are* looking at it.

Every *five fucking minutes*, it seems.

(Six thousand words in and we get the first use of the f-word - which is surprising, as I use it all the time. Anyone who says swearing is a sign of a small vocabulary needs kick in the head... a kick in the *fucking* head, that is.)

Can you sense my frustration with time keeping here? I'm sure you probably can.

I hate living according to a little round white face with numbers on and I'm sure if you think about it, you probably do too.

See what I did there?

Here I am moaning about time governing our lives and that we're all reliant on the clock - and I cheekily pop in a time-check to underline my point, contradicting myself in the process.

My English tutor always said I contradicted myself too much when I wrote an opinion piece, and here I am proving him right once more.

His name was Professor Wrigley and he always considered me to be something of a hack.

This was fine by me as it was the hacks who earned all the money, while the writing elite lived in misery - permanently half-way through a bottle of scotch, moaning incessantly about *the work* to anyone in earshot.

I bet they never spent their time glancing up at the nearest Timex though, seeing how long it was until lunch break.

No, for them I expect it was all about wandering through quaint street bazaars in Morocco, chatting up the local girls and writing down spurious observations on the nature of man's soul.

...I may have just alienated all the Hemingway fans with that little observation.

So the clock is our natural enemy. An evil deity controlling our lives on a day to day basis.

We even build bloody monuments to it, like the Tower of Westminster in London (and I do love the fact Big Ben is part of a building where the art of wasting time has really been *perfected* over the centuries).

Strange then, that the clock's nearest time monitoring relative, the calendar, makes us feel *good* about ourselves.

I'll grant you there are some things we put in a calendar that cause us heartache and stress. Dentist appointments for instance, or birthdays for relatives we hate but must buy a present for, otherwise our mothers will be cross with us for rocking the family boat.

How about the return to school date, after the long, lazy months of summer with nothing to do but watch TV, worry old people and vandalise bus shelters?

The whole point of looking at a calendar though, is that things tend to be quite *far off* and not looming round the corner, like a psychopath wearing a hockey mask.

29

Calendars can be safely ignored when necessary.

You may have one hanging in your kitchen - one of those long ones with pictures of slightly worried looking kittens on it - all those nasty appointments scrawled on it in biro, but at least you can avoid looking at the thing if needs be when you go to get a yoghurt out of the fridge.

When you're out of the kitchen entirely, it doesn't exist at all!

Out of sight, out of mind.

Not like mister clock however - who's impossible to get away from.

He's on your wrist, on the car dashboard, on the wall at work, in the bottom right hand corner of the computer screen.

Bastard!

He's everywhere, and no matter how hard you try, you'll eventually find yourself staring up and realising with horror that you've only got twenty minutes to finish the shopping before the kids get out of school.

Calendars also have good things written on them frequently. Things you want to remember.

Like holidays and the birthdays of relatives you do like - or your own, of course.

We all make sure we write down good things in **large black marker pen** so they're easy to see, drawing our attention away from the date of the next rectal exam just below.

I have a theory that men are bad at remembering things such as anniversaries and special occasions because most of them tend to go for calendars featuring naked women. Staring at a pair of big tits is a great diversion from the mother-in-law's birthday next Wednesday.

I have a calendar hanging in this room.

It's one of those dull corporate ones from some printing company or other.

I stole it from work because it has fairly large spaces to write in under the dates and covers up the hole I made during an aborted shelf-making incident.

Currently, a picture of a speedboat - looking very impressive as it carves its way through the surf - is being used to denote the fact it's April.

I have no idea why.

I guess spring must be a good time for a sixty-knot blow job through the harbour.

The calendar has only two entries on it for the month:

The first is my son's birthday - in **large black marker pen** - and the second is for a doctor's appointment - in small blue biro.

Here's a piece of advice: never keep a diary. *Ever.*

It will plague your existence and cause your sanity to slip from its moorings.

You start off with the best of intentions, carefully writing in every appointment and occasion in its clean, ordered pages and for a while at least, you'll stick to it.

Every appointment will be kept, you'll turn up on time for all meetings and everyone will think you're efficient and in control.

Then you'll lose the nasty bastard.

Because you've squirreled all that vital information away between the diary's faux leather cover and not committed any of it to memory, you won't have a bloody clue what it is you're supposed to be doing, or where you're supposed to be going.

You'll miss meetings, forget special occasions and everyone will conclude you've become addicted to prescription drugs and started to smell funny.

Years ago, I had one of those diaries with a calculator in it - stuck right next to the page for phone numbers.

Why it was there, I have no idea.

Perhaps you were meant to use it to multiply all the phone numbers together and arrive at the meaning of life.

The calculator worked for a week before leaking liquid crystal all over the diary, perhaps in an effort to highlight the futility of its own existence.

I got the thing for Christmas one year from an absent-minded uncle, who memorably also once bought me a vegetarian cookery book, along with a cardboard tube that made a mooing noise when you turned it upside down. I think it was some kind of cow calling device. I still have it somewhere, because every so often I need to take it out and have a look, to prove to myself I didn't dream the whole thing up.

I think my uncle's presents are the only ones I truly look forward to at Christmas these days.

I've received some extraordinarily silly presents in my time.

I seem to have one of those personalities where people think I like quirky and strange gifts, normally purchased from gadget shops.

Would you believe a friend once bought me a kite? When I was *thirty two*?

I'm all for staying young at heart, but do I really need to express it by running round the park on a windy day, trying to get a kite in the air for more than three seconds?

There I am on my birthday, wondering how long it will be until my hair falls out of my head, grows on my arse and gets thicker in my ears - and I unwrap a gift more suited for a time when I was as hairy as a cue ball and still thought Batman was real.

The epithet written on the card that came with the kite said:

'For when you want to get high!'

Stunning.

The kite went in the shed and I conveniently 'lost' the friend's phone number for a while.

My mother suggested I should keep the kite somewhere safe for my son.

Tom at this point was three months old and crapping himself was a regular and enjoyable activity, so I thought hoarding the kite for ten years was probably a waste of time.

Because I'm a writer, I tend to get presents related to that pursuit. Nothing useful though, like a new keyboard to replace the one I've broken the letter B on, or a book telling me how to write a best seller.

No, I get bought *quirky* things.

Like a pen with a radio in it.

Yes… a *pen* with a *radio* in it.

How desperate for friends have you got to be before that sounds like something you'd actually want?

Small earphones extended from the pen on a cable, which was slightly too short to be used without bending your head over to one side, looking like you were a tad mental.

I gather the person who bought it for me - a relative this time, so no chance of severing ties - thought I might enjoy the chance to write flowing script and listen to the radio at the same time, all from one convenient device.

And who could blame them? After all, it's not like it's possible to do those things easily and efficiently any other way, right?

Hmmm…

Singing socks.

They were a good one.

You put the socks on, pressed a button on the side and they warbled a tune at you. The song in question was 'Tiger Feet' by Mud (which is available on Spotify, I believe).

The socks had a badly stitched picture of a tiger on them. The small electronic device that controlled the whole thing rubbed irritatingly against your skin.

I wore them - once - for the delight and edification of my wife, who found the whole thing hilarious.

I can't really blame her. There I was, standing in my new socks, with a seventies rock song wafting from around my ankles and a green flannel dressing gown covering my modesty.

The expression on my face could best be described as *perplexed*.

At this point, it'd be nice to launch into a tirade about the companies who produce this crap.

I'd like nothing more than to vilify the fools who sit in product meetings and decide upon the latest crazes to fill our shops from floor to ceiling and drain our bank accounts with frightening rapidity.

But I can't do that because it's not really their fault.

It's *ours*.

The simple fact is, if we didn't keep buying this crap then they wouldn't keep making it. If we didn't keep buying pens with radios, singing socks, cardboard moo machines - or any one of a thousand other completely useless items you'll find in the shops - then these people would stop producing them. They'd then find more constructive things to do with their time, like inventing flasks that keep the contents hot, or office chairs that don't make your arse numb.

Have you noticed the kind of stores that sell this stuff only exist for a short period of time before disappearing into the ether?

They usually spring up at Christmas in otherwise disused shops, promising quality presents at rock bottom prices. They're generally manned by people who are on day release from minimum security, or haven't been caught by the police yet.

They tend to get out of town long before you come back, wanting to complain about how the novelty indoor fountain you bought for your auntie Jenny has stopped working and started making disturbing farting noises in the middle of the night.

There are many reasons why we keep buying these weird and wonderful gifts, but mainly it's because they make Christmas shopping a whole lot easier.

Unless you're buying for children - who are happy with anything, provided it's plastic, brightly coloured and incredibly expensive - it's hard to come up with gifts that aren't as dull as ditch-water.

I'm as guilty of it as anybody.

My father is the kind of man who's always had the money to buy what he wants and the sense to know what he doesn't. Therefore, purchasing presents that elicit any kind of positive or heart-felt appreciation is next to impossible.

This makes the Christmas Eve shopping trip even more of a nightmare.

———

The amount of time I've stood in front of the gifts section at Boots, wondering whether to buy dad a ceramic miniature garden gnome or bathroom set - you know, the ones that invariably contain shower gel, talc, deodorant and an amusingly shaped bar of soap - doesn't bear thinking about.

I've settled for the fairly stress free option of buying him a bottle of whisky every year. He may not appreciate it, but he's normally so pissed by the time I talk to him, it *sounds* like he does.

A small, guilty part of me thinks I'm turning him into a raging alcoholic. I'm convinced at some point he's going to decide I'm trying to kill him in order to get my hands on an inheritance.

I might swap to cigars in the next couple of years. Give his liver a rest and his lungs a wake up call.

My mother, bless her, is grateful for whatever I buy and I love her for it. She keeps *everything*.

There's a dusty box in her bedroom closet that contains Christmas cards written by me at the age of seven.

I had a look through them once. It disturbed me that my handwriting hasn't improved much.

Much like my father, I have a distinct inability to show gratitude when I receive an unwanted or ridiculous gift. I have a big problem with what I like to call the *post-unwrap pause*.

This is the time when you've successfully unwrapped the present enough to see what it is and registered the fact it's the worst present in history. You then have to fake a look of gratitude at the wizened old carbuncle of a grandmother who bought it for you.

It's very difficult.

I find myself making a rather high-pitched keening noise, accompanied by my face twisting horrendously into something approximating joy and surprise.

I'll then come out with a comment along the lines of:

'Oh! Thank you, Gran! I was just thinking the other day it'd be nice to write and listen to the radio at the same time.'

To me, I sound about as convincing as Hermann Goering's defence lawyer at the Nuremberg trials, but she seems to take what I'm saying at face value, concludes the festive transaction with a kiss, and a short anecdote about how she was passing The Gadget Shop, saw the offending item in the window and immediately thought of me.

It's a lot easier to open presents when the giver isn't in the room with you. You can safely express your feelings about the quality and suitability of your new possession by swearing at it, or burying it at the bottom of the garden beneath the miniature gnome.

Bearing this in mind, I've resolved to open my annual Christmas haul from now on in the toilet with the door locked.

I tend to find shopping in general to be something of a trial, even if it's for me.

This is particularly true when I'm hunting around for a large, expensive item, like a car or holiday.

The more money you're spending, the more stressful the job becomes, because you know it's a big decision. You've saved for months and want to know you're getting your money's worth, don't you?

I have virtually no problem with small stuff, like scanning the racks of HMV for a blu-ray, or picking out a new pair of jeans in the Gap.

Big items are a totally different matter.

Time for another anecdote:

I'm thirty two and thinking of buying a new car.

The Volvo I've been nursing around for eight years has finally reached the end of its days. I know this because every time I turn the steering wheel, it knocks like the knees of a nervous chorus girl.

When I switch the engine off, the whole car makes a dispirited groaning noise, before settling back on its worn suspension like an old man collapsing into his arm chair after a hard day's shuffleboard with the lads down the working men's club.

I buy all the right car magazines and pour through them, looking at pages and pages of automobiles.

I talk to my wife, telling her all about the type of car I'd like, showing her pictures I've ringed with a highlighter.

There's something in the male psychology that responds to the internal combustion engine - even men like me, who have little or no appreciation of how the thing works.

My wife looks at the highlighted cars, listens calmly to me going on about the one I want and then tells me the type of car I'm actually going to *have*.

I want a sports car you see, one with fat tyres and an engine that sounds like a lion with a chicken bone stuck in its throat.

Something vaguely resembling a penis would be corking, too…

My wife just wants one in a nice burgundy colour, reliable and cheap to run.

There's all the evidence you need for why men and women are very different creatures… and why women tend to win arguments like this.

With the options narrowed down to something burgundy and big enough to carry one man, one woman, one small child and the three tons of baby equipment that go with him, I set off for the local garages on a car hunting expedition.

It doesn't go well.

I find nothing I like in the budget I have - certainly nothing in burgundy anyway. I return home dispirited and contemplate another few months of nursing the Volvo around trying to ignore the knocking.

The next day, I try again.

The wife comes this time, automatically making it twice as bad an experience.

This is not to say she does anything wrong, it's just that:

Man + Woman in car for four hours with conflicting ideas = Hell on Earth.

Chuck the baby into the mixture and Hell on Earth can't even begin to describe it.

This day is a failure as well and I starting to twitch every time I drive past a burgundy car.

Eventually - at nearly five o'clock - we're preparing to go home.

I've smoked a pack of cigarettes, she's got a face like thunder and Tom has dropped a load in his shorts, making the Volvo not only drive like shit, but smell like it too.

We're headed in the direction of home, visiting one last garage on the way back. It's small, independently run, with only a tiny entry in the Yellow Pages.

We roll past it… and I spot automotive *Heaven*.

The car might as well have been surrounded in a halo of bright, white light with angels sitting on the bonnet waving at me.

A buzzing neon sign should have been hovering above it, saying *Buy me, Spalding!*

It's the car I want. The car I *must* have!

We'll leave me sat in the Volvo salivating for the moment to take a brief aside:

At that time in life – thirty two and a new father - I'm harbouring a desire for one of those cars corporate businessmen drive.

I've just started working at a marketing company and while I'm not massively swayed by the image thing, I feel something along the lines of a BMW or a Mercedes would give me the right kind of look that an important go-getting marketing superstar should have.

And there it sits!

Perfection - or as near to it as my bank balance will let me get.

It's a BMW 5 Series, up for the asking price of £6000.

While it's not burgundy, it is a deep shade of red. Close enough to please the wife's aesthetic sensibilities.

The squeal of the Volvo's brakes echo along the street as I turn sharply into the garage forecourt.

The sound of my wife's protests ring in my ears, forming a two-part harmony with the rapid-fire knocking of the Volvo's steering column. Tom begins crying in the back in great gasping wails.

The combined din creates a symphony of distress only a deaf person could love.

The Volvo bucks over a bump at the entrance and exhaust fumes billow out impressively. It's like something out of a really action-packed episode of 24 – without the shouting, complicated electronic gadgets and man bag.

I park the car - which groans as I turn the ignition off - and jump out like I'm auditioning for a part in a Bruce Willis movie.

The grin of a six year old boy spreads across my face as I approach the BMW (alright, I sprint up to it like an idiot) and take in its automotive majesty.

The wife gets out of the car, leaving Tom to wallow in the stench of his latest creation and comes to stand beside me, knowing full well getting much sense out of me is going to be like pulling teeth.

'You like it then?' she says, arms crossed and stoic expression on her face.

'Yeah. Yeah. I really do! It's fantastic!' says the six year old, trapped in my thirty two year old body.

'It's a bit pricey, isn't it?' she points out, a frown appearing.

'We can afford it. We can!' says mister six year old, his legs starting to tremble with excitement. 'Look! It's a BMW!'

'Yes, I can see that. What with the car's badge being two feet in front of me and everything.'

'I've always wanted a BMW!'

'Have you really? I'd never have guessed.'

My wife's thinly veiled sarcasm is lost on me as I begin to look around the car, checking all the things I can remember are important at times like this:

Rust on the bodywork and wheel arches, condition of the tyres, signs of welding... and so on and so forth.

I almost look as if I know what I'm doing to the casual observer.

I don't of course, but I can stroke my chin thoughtfully and tap bits of metal right up there with the best of them.

All practical considerations go right out the window when I look at the interior and spot the leather upholstery.

It looks extremely comfortable and it's large enough in there for a family of illegal immigrants to live in.

There also appears to be an on-board computer, which I can see myself playing with endlessly.

The car doesn't really look much like a penis and the tyres are only moderately fat, but I can already hear the growling engine note in my head.

The Germans make very good cars, there's no doubting that.

I came up with a Spalding Theory ™ on this a while back and here it is:

Horrendous War Crimes Equal Well Made Automobiles.

Think about it…

The Germans - instigators of two world wars and some of the worst cruelty ever inflicted by man, and the Japanese - who tortured POWs, made forced labour marches and butchered half of China in the 1930s.

Both countries produce attractive, well built motor cars:

BMW, Audi, Mercedes, Volkswagon, Honda, Mitsubishi, Subaru, Nissan.

This is opposed to the so called 'good guys' of world conflict, who do the exact opposite.

The Americans produce wallowing trifles on wheels that suck gas and can't take a corner. The French make cars that are largely plastic, have trim that falls off in five minutes and break down nearly as quickly.

And as for the British motor industry… I think that was declared clinically dead in 1985. If you've ever driven an Austin Montego, I pity you and can recommend some excellent therapists.

I don't know if any of this is relevant, but it's something to ponder, eh?

Regardless of how the Germans behaved in the war, they make a damn fine BMW 5 Series. The Bavarian Motor Works company have really come up trumps on this one.

I want this car. I want it *now!*

'We'd better find someone,' says the wife, consigned to the fact her husband has regressed twenty four years and a BMW will soon be sitting on the driveway.

As if on cue, out saunters the salesman. He's dressed in a suit bought for too much money off the rack, a pair of the shiniest shiny shoes you've ever seen and an orange tan from his two weeks contracting STDs in Ibiza.

He has a look in his eye.

The kind usually reserved for big game hunters when they spot the last elephant in the area minding its own business at the waterhole.

'Hello there, sir. Can I help you?'

Well of course you can help me you idiot! You can make my dreams come true!

'Yes. I think you can. I'm interested in this BMW.' I'm trying to sound cool. I'm trying to sound aloof. I'm trying to sound like an adult. And I'm nearly succeeding. All that's ruining the effect is that my voice has gone up a couple of octaves and I'm jigging back and forth on the spot like a morris dancer with haemorrhoids.

'Yeah? Good choice, sir. It's only been on the forecourt for a day. Already got someone interested in it, but I'm sure we can come to an arrangement, sir.'

He may be saying *sir* but he's thinking *chump*.

He's smiling like the Cheshire cat.

He's metaphorically rubbing his hands together and laughing like a villain from a Batman comic.

To him, I look like a giant lemon holding a fistful of money.

I notice none of this.

We then proceed to have a very manly discussion.

We talk of previous owners and mileage. We expound at length on service history and reliability.

He tells me the car is *genuine* and *honest*, like he's describing the characteristics of a man he met in a bar and not a lump of inanimate metal.

I nod my head sagely and remark on how the Germans always make good cars, despite their international human rights record.

My wife has by this time returned to the car, where she's trying to entertain my rapidly tiring son.

The salesman suggests a test drive. I nod so hard it gives me a headache.

I persuade the wife to come along, so she can share in the glory of the leather upholstery and smooth ride.

The salesman gives me the keys and we all pile in.

I ignore the anxious looks he keeps throwing at my son on the back seat. He's no doubt terrified that at any moment Tom is going to vomit all over the BMW's expensive leather interior. I could've assured him that if it were ever going to happen, it would only be well after I'd bought the car and the family was two hundred miles up the M25 on a bank holiday weekend.

I start the engine and it purrs into life.

Driving out of the forecourt I feel like a king and proceed to drive the BMW around the local area, resisting the impulse to wave graciously at passers-by.

During all of this I don't even think to ask any questions, or check the quality of the electrics, suspension, lights or gears. I'm totally mesmerised by the lovely LCD on-board computer display, the miles-per-gallon gauge and the power steering.

I ask my wife if she'd like a go. She gives me an expression that speaks volumes and I let it pass.

We return safely to the forecourt, the grin on my face now so big the top of my head is in danger of falling off with a wet plop.

We get out and I inexplicably give the car a gentle pat on the bonnet. The salesman notes this and pound signs start floating in front of his eyes.

We then start to haggle.

This is where problems occur…

I can't haggle. I'm useless at it.

I'm the type of person who likes to have a price staring them straight in the face from the get-go, with no chance of variation. Life is much simpler, and transactions proceed with a smoothness I adore.

The prospect of standing toe to toe with someone who is no doubt infinitely better at haggling than I am makes me nauseous.

The term *or nearest offer* fills me with dread.

Even using Ebay makes me break out in a cold sweat.

My new salesman friend begins the process by saying the car can't go for less than £5,900. I say I'll chuck in the Volvo as part exchange. He says that'll knock off the paltry sum of a hundred quid, which shows he has enough talent at the car game to recognise a dying dog when he sees it.

I say it's only ten years old and has got to be worth at least two hundred.

He looks at me in disgust.

Distress and panic set in.

Any hold I have over the negotiations flies out of the window and I start to make truly idiotic bids.

I tell him I'll give him three grand for the car. *Half its value.*

He laughs, tells me I'm winding him up and reiterates the previous offer. I've already forgotten about using the Volvo as part exchange and counter with the genius bid of £5,850, thus putting myself another fifty quid out of pocket.

He looks stunned by this and starts to back away.

I stare at him for an uncomfortable amount of time before lowering my eyes and shuffling my feet.

It's all going away from me at this point.

I'm so out of my depth I'm bumping into sperm whales and giant squid.

Floundering, I do the only thing at this point that might save my bacon… I call the wife over.

***

She comes, arms folding across her chest, taking in the situation with one glance. Knowing her husband and knowing what has to be done, she talks to the salesman and I melt into the background, feigning an interest in the condition of the alloy wheels.

My wife starts her own method of negotiating, which is to speak in the same low, monotonous tone and stare directly into the salesman's eyes. It's like watching a mongoose sizing up a snake.

Some time passes and I surface from my detailed alloy inspection to be told that we can have the car for £5,500 and absolutely no less.

I nod my head enthusiastically and delve into my pocket for my wallet, like I'm going to produce the cash there and then. I'm stopped by my wife and told we have to go into the salesman's office to sort out the paperwork. This sinks in and I return the wallet in a hurry.

As my wife goes to collect Tom, I notice the salesman getting a good eyeful of her bottom. I instantly understand why we got five hundred quid off the car, and why all negotiations with salesman of any kind will henceforth be done by her.

Some thirty minutes later I emerge from the office in dreamy contentment.

I own a BMW.

With the key fob in my hand, I float towards my new acquisition on a wave of happiness. My wife and the salesman exchange parting pleasantries. He remarks on how sweet Tom is and she wishes him a nice rest of the weekend. Tom looks up from his kiddie seat with dribble around his mouth and a wide eyed smile.

Twenty feet away, his father looks exactly the same.

I press the alarm activator on the key fob. The alarm goes *beep beeeeeeep beeep*, the doors unlock and the lights flash.

I'm in Heaven.

I continue to stay in nirvana as we drive away from the salesman - who knows he's just sold a five thousand pound car for five hundred quid extra - and set off for home.

I take a really, really long route.

For the next month, the sound of the alarm activating or de-activating will give me a little thrill every time I hear it. I'll occasionally look at the car from the front window of my house and will spend more time than is necessary on a Sunday morning cleaning it.

I don't mind the fact that my bank balance is now a hell of a lot smaller, or that my petrol consumption has sky rocketed. My friends at work like the car and I can tell they're all just a bit jealous.

Everywhere I go, I drive upright and proud, grinning all the time.

The car may not look like a penis, but I more than make up for that by looking like one myself while I drive it.

The car won't start to have problems for nearly a year and a half, and by that time I have far larger concerns.

Namely, the increasing likelihood that my wife - who so neatly stepped into fill the breach on that garage forecourt - is going to divorce me.

That ended on a bit of a down note, didn't it?

Sorry about that.

I didn't intend it to, but these things happen.

I'll be honest with you, I considered deleting the last paragraph to finish the story on a high, but then decided against it. After all, I said I was going to be honest with you and that's what came out on the page.

You may be wondering what went wrong with my wife and I promise to get to it before this book is done.

I'm going to leave it for a while though, if you don't mind. It's the kind of thing I need a good run up to.

So, how are we doing as the night drags on and these chairs deaden the feeling in our posteriors?

Not too bad I think, not too bad at all.

I'm still feeling pretty fresh. Still up for some rock n' roll.

Hope you are too.

It looks like I've still got your attention and that's a very good thing.

By this point in a book the reader has pretty much decided whether they're enjoying themselves, and will probably stick it out to the end if they are.

Our friendship is growing all the time and it looks like you've relaxed in my company.

*Look...*you've taken off your shoes and put your feet on the desk. Both good signs that you're content.

There might be aspects you'd change if you could, I'm sure.

You might occasionally blanch at the language I use, the metaphors and analogies I'm employing, or the way I construct my paragraphs - but on the whole you're pretty happy with the big picture.

As a writer, that's nice to know. It massages my fragile ego nicely.

All writers have fragile egos to one extent or another.

Writers like me - who haven't reached the giddy heights of fame and fortune - tend to have the most fragile of all.

Anyone who works in the creative arts tends to suffer from it. It's part of the job.

Actors, painters, singers, dancers and writers: we're all basically hoping what we do is appreciated, enjoyed and above all *wanted.*

When I'm writing, it's coming from the heart, so when you get rejections or knock backs, it hits home heavily.

Every story I write - everything I put on the page - is personal. And pretty life consuming while I'm writing it.

You'd like to think you were creating a masterpiece, but there's a part of you more likely to worry it's a disaster of epic proportions.

I call this the *black little voice*, which chips in every once in a while and makes you doubt yourself.

It's very important to ignore him, as he'll drive you crazy.

Some people try to drown him out with drink or drugs. I prefer to ignore him the way you tune out interference on the radio when a song comes on that you like. I only resort to intoxicants when the knob breaks off.

Quick, let's move on as fast as possible, so he doesn't notice what's happening and ruin the flow I've got going...

Every writer is emotionally attached to their work, so when you send your baby out into the world for analysis and appraisal, you're filled with a strange combination of dread and mindless optimism.

You hope the little fella will stand on his sturdy little legs and walk in a straight line, without bumping into the furniture too much. You know you won't be able to stand behind him with your arms outstretched, ready to catch him if he falls, so you spend an anxious time waiting to hear a cry of startled pain or gurgle of excitement.

This is otherwise known as *feedback*.

I guess that's why I decided to take this project on.

At least I'll only spend a short amount of time on it, so if nobody likes it the blow will be far easier to deal with. No harm, no foul. Only a weekend lost.

The labour will be over quickly and the delivery won't be too exhausting.

Besides, I'm actually enjoying this immensely. It beats watching Lost repeats any day.

Having said all that stuff about fragile egos and rejections, let's not get it out of proportion, shall we?

There's nothing worse than listening to some arty type, tragically bemoaning their lack of success, the long hours they've put in *suffering* for their art, and how under appreciated they feel.

When I talk to folks like that, I have a fancy to line up some junior doctors, policemen and firemen while they're gabbing away about not being appreciated - and let them pound on their stupid faces for a couple of hours.

I first discovered a desire - and a degree of talent I'd like to think - for writing at school. English classes were always my favourite, despite being sat next to a rather obnoxious fat boy called Clive, who liked to pick his nose with my Star Wars pencil.

I was thirteen and had a BMX - which was the coolest thing in the world.

I remember we were given a project to create an outline for a book we'd like to write. To me, this sounded like a fantastic idea and I threw myself into it with abandon.

The TV was switched off, the pencils were sharpened to a lethal point and the BMX was left out in the garden, one wheel spinning forlornly in the breeze.

Four weeks later my masterpiece was complete.

I'd been reading Tolkien's The Lord Of The Rings and was heavily influenced by it, so my project was a searing epic full of wizards, magic and dubious plot developments.

I thought it was *wonderful.*

It had maps and character descriptions. It had a run down of the plot and a detailed back story. It was the blueprint for a novel so epic, it'd make The Bible look like a pamphlet. It was a labour of love.

I handed it to the teacher - who looked a little worried by the size of it - and wandered off to buy sweets, secure in the knowledge an A grade was on the cards.

'Twas not to be.

In the end, I received a D - because the teacher felt it was too long and didn't conform to the assignment we'd been given. And she was right.

We were told to write two thousand words.

I'd written nearly *twenty five* thousand.

Including all the folded maps I'd drawn, the thing was enormous. I had to carry a bowling ball under my left arm to balance the weight of my school bag under the right.

I took the D with the kind of grace and acceptance any thirteen year old would demonstrate. I stormed home with a face like thunder, kicked the cat and snapped the arms off all my Star Wars action figures.

I got my first taste of rejection at a young age, but the disappointment didn't hold me back or depress me for too long.

It was that wonderful time of life where let-downs are usually forgotten about once the cartoons come on.

My mother wasn't quite so pleased when she found out I'd failed the assignment and the cartoons were withheld in no uncertain terms for a couple of weeks.

As I reached my late teens, I found my capacity for invention on the page was, if not quite limitless, then at least relatively prolific and I started to write more, convinced a best seller was just around the corner.

Everything I wrote was crap, of course.

At eighteen years old, you like to think you've already arrived at all the answers to the important questions in life, and have a solid and unshakable belief you're great and the rest of the world just doesn't know it yet.

I would sit for seemingly endless hours perched on a chair (nowhere as comfortable as this one) tapping away on a rapidly aging electronic typewriter, which was slower than the shifting continental plates and needed its ink ribbon changing nearly every day.

I was fully convinced I was creating masterpieces at every turn. That my prose was blinding, my observations striking, my characters well-rounded and my plots Machiavellian in their brilliance.

In reality, what I was writing were bad knock-offs of the authors I liked at the time:

James Herbert writes a book about killer rats, I write a short story about killer hedgehogs. It was called 'Spine Slaughter' (and you can grab an updated version of it at Amazon if you like).

Robert Ludlum writes about a secret agent with no memory, I write about a covert ops soldier with no memory.

And so it went on.

Ream after ream of rubbish.

Page after page of recycled plot devices and one-dimensional characters, displaying no originality *whatsoever*.

I would have made a great Hollywood studio executive…

You may think I'm being hard on myself but trust me, I'm not.

Memorably, one of my stories started with this particular piece of astounding prose - original grammar included:

'He was dead, and he knew it. His lungs were ruptured, and his brains leaked, all over the road. He'd received the bullets straight into his body without screaming, as any man of his mettle should do.'

See what I mean?
Horrific.
How the hell do you 'receive a bullet'?
Was it gift wrapped in a bow and sent from an absent-minded uncle?
Terrible, terrible stuff.

At the time I thought it was potentially award winning.

The ego was swiftly knocked out of me as I started to send some material out for consideration.

I'm sure it was considered... considered a good substitute for the tea-coaster on the editor's desk, that is.

I must have posted out roughly seventy or eighty copies of my dreadful short stories, film scripts and novellas, before finally getting the message that I was either monumentally untalented, or so far up my own arse I could see the plaque on the back of my teeth.

The desire to continue dwindled and I put my writing on semi-permanent hold.

I did quite a lot of writing at university, as most students do, but it was all flowery hogwash. A lot of pretentious observations on the rise of the post-modernist text in contemporary literature, or the role of hegemony within 18th century fiction. The kind of stuff only utter tossers would read outside the confines of an undergraduate degree. So while I'd put the writing career on hold *per se*, I still hadn't managed to remove my head from my arse.

Anyway, three years of university rolled by and despite soiling myself in front of my peers, it was a hugely enjoyable experience.

I won't bore you with tales of these years, as one man's university experience is more or less the same as another's:

Essays, drinking too much, waffling lecturers, pretentious conversations in seminars, sex with anaemic art students... that kind of malarkey.

At the end of my degree (if you're really interested, I walked out with a 2.1) I went into full time employment and found it *very* boring indeed.

I needed something to keep the old synapses functioning, to prevent them drying up like a worm caught in the mid-day sun. So I returned to writing, armed with a bit more life experience and more big words in my vocabulary.

What I wrote was better than my teenage efforts - if not by much.

Bad rip-offs were replaced by original stories, but I did have a tendency to use too many words.

Where only a brief description was needed, I would launch into verbose and obese sentences that sounded convoluted and meant nothing.

Here's an example:

'The tenuous link the restaurant had to the halcyon days of yesteryear were exemplified by its archetypal furnishings and nostalgic uniforms.'

Gah.

If I wrote that sentence now, it would read:

'The restaurant looked like it did in 1958.'

Yet again, I sent my product off to literary agents and publishers - and yet again received countless rejections. All of them as valid as the one I got for the psychopathic hedgehog story several years previously.

Malaise set in once again and the Writer's and Artists Yearbook went back into mothballs.

To fill the gap, I started amateur dramatics with a local company, and played a particularly fine country bumpkin in that year's pantomime Mother Goose.

I thought acting was easy.

I later learned it was *pantomimes* that were easy and proper acting - in proper plays with proper characters - was most definitely *not*.

There's nothing quite like drying on stage during Death Of A Salesman to let you know you're probably not cut out for the stage.

Remember we talked about time and how it goes slower when you're not enjoying yourself?

Well, time stops *completely* when you walk on stage, forget your lines and see an ocean of faces squinting up at you, expecting their money's worth.

It eventually took a panicked member of the stage crew to whisper the line to me, which I delivered in a voice so strangled the audience thought my character had been poisoned.

When the play ended, I removed my costume, went straight to the nearest pub and proceeded to blot the incident out - with remarkable success.

With my acting career buried in an unmarked shallow grave, I turned once again to literary pursuits.

Not quite like the last time, though.

I thought I'd try a spot of journalism and started writing non-fiction for a variety of magazines. These stories were short, to the point, contained no flowery words and were all my own work.

I sold three in six months.

I made a grand total of two hundred and fifty quid on all of them, but it felt like I'd made two hundred and fifty *thousand*.

I'd found something of a niche for myself and intended to exploit it. Opportunity knocked when my girlfriend of the time - who'd later become my wife - cut out a clipping from the jobs section of the local paper, advertising for a copy-writer at a marketing firm.

It was one of those companies who get jobs in from clients, knock up the required advertising copy and charge extortionate amounts of money for the privilege.

I liked the job as soon as I got it.

And I still do.

I've worked there ever since and my need to write is serviced by the material I produce.

Chances are you've read some of it yourself - if you're in the UK, anyway.

Every so often I'll catch a glimpse of my work in a magazine or on a billboard and a feeling of pride will wash over me.

The only thing wrong with writing this way - thinking up copy for marketing purposes - is that it tends to be quite soulless.

When you work in marketing you're essentially bullshitting for a living...

The job of the marketer is to sell the product and nothing else.

Never mind if said product has been recalled to the factory six times, or independent research has shown it breaks after more than ten uses. Your job is to make it sound like it's the best thing since sliced bread and that every home should have one. Or even two, if you're *very* good.

It may go against all your instincts to say that this brand new vacuum cleaner is so powerful it can change the axis of the earth's rotation, but you'd better damn well put it down on paper like the client asks - otherwise you might find yourself with a P45 and a future likely to suck harder than the vacuum actually does.

It only takes a while before this has a negative affect on your creative output.

I was getting to the point where the whole thing was depressing me more and more - when I woke up one Saturday morning with the idea to write a book in one sitting.

Which brings us bang up to date, doesn't it?

Writing the right thing - clumsy sentence structure there, my humblest apologies - is sometimes crucial to the success of a product and sometimes not, but writing the *wrong* thing can be a disaster of epic proportions.

I was nearly sacked a couple of years ago because of a missing L in copy I'd written and proof checked before sending to print.

The text was for a large metropolitan college, who'd paid a king's ransom for a prospectus that would amaze and delight anyone who happened to pick it up for a nose through.

It was a stunning combination of amazing photography, showing how great the college's facilities were (faked) and equally brilliant copy about how its courses were far, far better than anyone else's (lie).

One of the subjects this thing advertised was Public Services.

A course that existed - as far as I could tell - to teach the young people of today how to be the soldiers of tomorrow. Which no doubt involved learning how to drink too much beer, pick fights with the night club bouncers and catch gonorrhoea from the local prostitutes.

Now you know the title of the course, I'm sure you can work out why that missing L caused such a fuss.

Yes, a hundred thousand copies of this weighty tome went to the local populace, and emblazoned in bold Helvetica font on page 48 was the course information for:

Pubic Services.
Two-Year Course.
Learn all about this fascinating area and prepare yourself for a job in the field!

Oh dear.

There were phone calls, there were meetings, there were arguments in hallways. It really is incredible how one letter can cause a catastrophe of such magnitude.

I personally thought a two year course spent delving around in someone else's genital region sounded quite appealing, but I was in the minority. It would be the type of course any aspiring pornographic film star would have jumped at the chance to be on.

I was called to my manager's office like a naughty school boy who'd been caught wiping bogeys on the class hamster.

He proceeded to tell me - at length - about the importance of proof reading and how mistakes like this can damage the company's reputation.

For my part, I sat there silently, desperately trying not to laugh as he described how the principal had rung him wanting to know why we were selling his college as the kind of place that encouraged sexual deviance.

...it could have been worse though.

I could have accidentally added a letter F to the Performing Arts section of the prospectus, which would have had the college advertising:

Performing Farts.
Two year course.
Improve your skills and entertain the public.

I managed to talk my way out of that mess in the end.
I passed the buck successfully onto the printing department.

It wasn't difficult as they're a strange bunch down there - all cross-eyed and twitchy. The ink fumes addle their brains over a long enough period of time, I'm led to believe.

God may have cursed me with a brain that gets me into trouble, but he also blessed me with a mouth that can get me out of it again.

I've always been very careful with proof reading since then and I make sure my writing never contains any silly spelling mestakes.

Blimey, it's getting late.

I was going to mention when midnight passed (and make some half-arsed gag about it, probably) but shot straight past it without remembering.

I'm pretty happy about that, it means horrible old mister clock is losing his grip on me as I get further into the book.

With any luck, I'll have forgotten about him completely by the end and will live the rest of my life in the peace and tranquillity of the relaxed and inattentive.

In the meantime… it's now Sunday, the day of rest.

No rest for Mrs Spalding's little boy, though.

He's still got a lot to say and hopefully the time to do it. I suppose it all depends on that bastard on the wall.

How are you doing as we head through the night?

I've bumped the heating up a bit as there's nothing more annoying than catching a chill in the wee small hours.

There are some blankets in the airing cupboard and you're more than welcome to drape one across your legs if you like.

I've refilled the coffee thermos, so there's plenty of caffeine to keep the eyes open and brain awake. I'd hurry up and drink it though, it'll be stone cold again in a few minutes. I own the world's only anti-thermos. It keeps cold stuff hot and hot stuff cold.

…can you hear those people outside?

Noisy aren't they?

They must be coming home from a night's heavy drinking - making the kind of commotion that annoys the brave and frightens the timid.

Don't worry, they'll be past the window soon and well on their way home to bed, where they'll sleep the sleep of the just.

The just about to throw up that is…

Then they'll wake up tomorrow morning in the safe and secure knowledge it's Sunday and the pain of getting up for work is still a day away.

Nobody likes work. *No-one.*

I don't care if you're Brad Pitt and you're making a movie where you spend the entire running time having naked lap dancers caress your body.

I don't care if you're Bill Gates and you spend five minutes a day looking at specs for a new hard drive and three hours playing tennis with the guys from Intel.

No matter what job you do, there's always a frisson of dread accompanying the sound of that infernal alarm going off at 6.30am on Monday morning.

You may not feel the dread too much if you happen love your job, but it's still there – deep down where the animal in you just wants to roll over and go back to sleep.

The Chinese have a saying that goes:

'Find a job you love and you'll never work a day in your life.'

Spalding has a saying that goes:

'Find a job you love and the groan escaping your lips at the crack of dawn will be quieter.'

For most of us, the groan is usually *quite bloody loud*, because we're not movie stars or multi-millionaire business moguls.

We're ordinary working folk, who live by the clock and have to obey that hateful ritual of rising when the birds are delivering the morning chorus.

We shuffle around like zombies until we've had our cup of tea and bowl of Cornflakes - or Bran Flakes if we're not, you know, *regular* - which wake up the brain cells enough to negotiate the shower and the complicated business of getting dressed.

The shower lasts for five minutes, but seems like five seconds and getting dressed is unnecessarily difficult because most of the clothes we're wearing today were left turned inside out in a heap on the floor last night.

...although that last problem could just be mine. I'm a messy sod, I admit.

Then off we go!

To our place of work, where we spend more hours a week than anywhere else and sometimes think we might as well bring a sleeping bag in and cut out the middle man.

It's not natural. None of it is.

We're supposed to be hunter-gathers.

We're supposed to rise when our body clocks tell us and spend the day in honest work, revolving around eating, fucking and raising our young.

These things are important. These things keep the human race functioning.

Spending your entire day thinking up new and exciting ways to sell expensive aftershave in funny shaped bottles to over-achieving twenty five year old men *isn't*.

The world isn't going to fall apart if we're not walking around smelling of African Musk or Cool Breeze, is it?

Is your job important?

Let's work it out:

In your line of work do you help to save the lives of others? Do you supply necessary and vital equipment or items? Do you help provide detailed and accurate information which aids your fellow man?

No?

Then your job isn't important and is the kind robots will be doing soon.

Please don't let it get you down - not for a second. After all, you're not the only one.

I'm certainly the same as you and look forward to the day when the BRUCE 5 Marketing Copy Robot - serial Number 6575-111# - takes over and makes me obsolete.

Then I can swan around Moroccan bazaars, chatting up the local girls and contemplate the nature of man's existence with a bottle of Jack Daniels by my side.

...I have a feeling the Hemingway references are doing me absolutely no favours.

Never mind, give it ten years and most of the classics will have been re-written by the ERNEST 12 Literary Genius Robot - serial Number 6575-7774#.

Does your job involve meetings? If so, I feel sorry for you and can whole-heartedly sympathise.

My life is a constant stream of one meeting after another, with clients and portly company chief executives.

They read everything you put in front of them with a look like they're sucking a large and bitter lemon, and all think being rich and portly means they have something valuable to contribute to the writing of promotional copy.

They're all dead wrong.

The amount of arguments I've had with the egotistical money-bags - who feel the word *smelltastic* should replace *aromatic* in my description of a cooking sauce - is ever increasing and ever more annoying.

I even have meetings about having meetings...

There was one occasion where I was called in for a meeting to decide what we would say to an important client at a *second* meeting - at which we would be preparing the agenda for a further meeting with the client's board of directors.

In essence: a meeting about a meeting about a *meeting*.

If I'm not having meetings, I'm attending conferences or workshops on how to run a business. You know, the type of thing that was invented in California twenty years ago and has insinuated itself on the rest of us in the intervening decades.

It's a miracle I ever get any work done.

There's one phrase that fills me with an irrational desire to twist the heads off human beings:

'There's no I in team!'

The classic phrase - invented by Californians - to denote the concept that everyone is working together towards a glorious outcome. One that will make us all rich and universally adored.

I hate it.

I hate it. I hate it. *I hate it.*

There's no I in team, but I think you'll find there are five A's in *'you're a Californian twat, pal'*.

It's the most idiotic, shallow and above all *untruthful* phrase ever invented.

It completely ignores human nature and the most fundamental aspects of our social personality.

We're not built to work in teams and forget our own needs for the greater good. We're built to strive as individuals. It's hard-wired into our brains and no amount of *positive thinking* blather will ever change that.

It's also an insidious piece of propaganda, designed to make the ordinary folk think they're benefiting - when all they're doing is stressing themselves out and lining the pockets of senior management.

Every year, thousands of reticent workers are forced to engage in team building exercises meant to promote a feeling of fellowship.

Never mind that Claire from Accounts hates Susan from Personnel with a passion that's almost holy because she stole her boyfriend Carlos.

Forget the fact that everyone in the office universally despises Colin, the rat-faced line manager, who only got the job because his father is *on the board*.

No, let's not worry about these things.

Instead, let's all go to a small Travel Inn in the Lake District for a weekend of *exciting group activities* and *fun co-operative exercises*.

Oh jolly, jolly bullcrap.

Nobody below senior management wants to go on these trips - and they only do because it gives them a chance to give the Jag a run up to the country.

Everyone has to though, as not going would mean forfeiting those days in lieu you've built up for the two weeks in Tenerife you promised the other half.

So you travel the three hours to the hotel with a sinking heart and a stress headache forming above your right eye.

…and you just know the person you'll be in the same hotel room as - because the company is too stingy to spring for a room each - will be Colin the line manager and his bizarre bathroom habits.

The weekend crawls by at roughly the speed of a stoned sloth.

You play the games you're required to and share some half-hearted jokes with the boss - who you know will fire you on sight if you don't get that processing report to him by Wednesday morning.

Everyone grins and bears the jobbing actors employed to be your *Team Leaders!* and you wind up getting totally bladdered in the hotel bar each night with the three or four people in your office you actually get along with.

The night is capped off by returning to your hotel room to find Colin on the toilet, cleaning his teeth and ear holes - with the same brush.

The weekend concludes and you gratefully return home to complain about the whole debacle to your spouse. They take it all in good grace for about half an hour, before screaming that they don't want to hear anymore about the trust exercise, where you had to catch the three hundred pound elephant from the typing pool, giving yourself terrible backache.

And you know what?

The following morning back at work:

Claire still hates Susan, everyone still hates Colin, the processing report still isn't done and you've developed a nasty rash from the poison ivy you fell into during the *Team Trek!* round Lake Windermere.

I genuinely feel sorry for the working folk who buy into this corporate brainwashing. They come back from the team weekend with a renewed sense of purpose and a positive attitude that *anything can get done if we all work together and communicate!*

They'll be the ones trying their hardest to haul the rest of us up to an acceptable standard and will spend vast swathes of time printing off well meaning motivational posters.

They'll also be the ones that stay late and work harder, only to discover in three months that their annual holiday has been cut by five days and the Christmas bonus has been cancelled so that Colin and his dad can go skiing in Colorado.

Speaking from personal experience, I was forced to go to a paint-balling day in the New Forest about a year ago. I was not happy with this turn of events, as I'd planned to visit friend of mine in Ireland, where much drinking of Guinness was in store.

As it was, I had to get up at 6.00am - on a bloody Saturday! - drive out to a cold and windy forest and strap on body armour that made me look like Arnold Schwarzenegger's anaemic cousin.

Then I was forced to run around holding a mean looking paint ball gun, trying my best to avoid the poison ivy while attempting to shoot that annoying prick from Deliveries in the testicles.

Give a man a gun - any gun, real or fake - and at some point he'll start to think he's Jack Bauer.

The red mist of battle will come down and he'll run around in a strange bow-legged crouch, shouting out commands like Tom Hanks in Saving Private Ryan.

This happened to me after about an hour of mincing around in my camouflage jacket and combat goggles.

In the space of a few seconds, the bored expression on my face disappeared as I realised that I had a gun, protective armour and carte blanche to shoot other people in the head.

Off I went, eyes narrowed to slits and heart pounding like a jack hammer.

I was well and truly *in the moment*, barking out commands to junior members of staff and taking crafty pot shots at people from a handily placed bush.

This all went supremely well - for a while.

I felt I was bagging my limit and enacting small and petty acts of revenge on those who had dared to drink from my coffee cup or steal post-it notes from my desk.

Then - as is inevitable in Spalding's life - things took an unfortunate turn.

At the event was our marketing team and sundry other individuals from the company's lower echelons, along with four or five important clients, whose accounts we were managing at the time.

Among these clients was a large, sweaty gentleman from a pharmaceutical company, who was paying us a six figure sum to write and design some promotional pamphlets for a new anti-flea pill for dogs his boffins had cooked up.

It had been impressed on us *in no uncertain terms* that said gentleman must be accorded every courtesy, to ensure the account was retained.

This extended to my direct superior telling all us grunts that if we saw our pill-pushing cash cow during the paint-ball event, we were to aim *high* and *wide*.

So there I am, squatting behind my bush in cunning concealment, blasting anything that moves in sickly orange paint splats. I'm a poor shot, so more trees have developed a covering of orange than fellow combatants, it has to be said.

Homing into view were four people, not obeying the laws of paint-ball in the slightest by walking out in the open and chatting like they were at a cocktail party.

Two men and two women - with no idea there was a nutter in the bushes twenty feet away with a bead on them and the cold, red mist of war destroying any semblance of rationality.

You should be a couple of steps ahead of me at this point and have already reached the conclusion that one of these innocent deer was the sweaty gentleman from *Drugs 'R Us*.

I cared nothing for this. My dander was up and my blood was at boiling point.

Ah ah! I thought to myself. *Easy pickings*.

I levelled the paint-ball gun at the wandering group and squeezed off a few shots. I think I shouted something along the lines of: *'Die, you scum sucking mothers!'* as well, but I can't remember clearly.

Most of the paint balls mercifully missed their targets by miles, but three hit home with an accuracy that would have made Clint Eastwood hang up his poncho.

One ball hit a woman on the thigh. She let out a yelp of surprise and pain and started to hop up and down like Zebedee at a pogo-stick competition. I later learned this was Matilda - fat sweaty gentleman's German personal assistant.

The other two balls slammed into fat sweaty gentleman on his considerable paunch and only slightly less chunky neck.

He made an *oofing* noise when the gut shot went in and a high-pitched screech when the shot to the neck hammered home. Both were a delight to my battle-hardened ears.

Partly in shock, partly in delight and partly with unholy rage, I leapt from my hiding place and ran over, wailing like a banshee and with every intention of finishing off the other two from point blank range.

Hmmm.

There's a moment of absolute clarity sometimes that hits you like a metaphorical bucket of cold water.

I got within five feet of my prey and looked at them properly for the first time.

Fat sweaty man was bent double, hand clasped to rapidly reddening neck. Matilda the Hun was now sat in the mud, rubbing her leg vigorously and crying. The other two were fussing around and were the first to realise their insane attacker had pounced, intent on a crushing victory.

I recognised mister fat and sweaty at once and the bucket of cold water got chucked over my head, extinguishing the battle rage instantaneously.

He looked up at me with an expression I could only hope to copy by ramming a baseball bat up my arse.

I started to babble apologies.

The effect was diminished by the fact I was still waving the paintball gun around in wide arcs. Realising I was apologising and threatening them at the same time, I chucked the gun on the ground as if it was a red hot poker.

The icing on the cake came when I tried to help fatso to his feet.

I took his plump hands in mine and wrenched him upwards.

I am eleven and a half stone. He exceeded this by about eight.

The laws of physics took over and he fell back, now with the added bonus of me body slamming onto him as I toppled over.

I disentangled myself from the mess still spouting apologies and retreated to a safe distance while my unfortunate victims sorted themselves out.

Once everyone was back on their feet, the now orange spattered pharmaceutical giant began to laugh off the incident in that oh-so-very British way:

'Ah ha ha. No harm done. Good shooting! It's all just a bit of fun isn't it?'

And so on.

I started laughing too. It was the kind of laugh insane people make in action movies before the hero blows them up.

We walked back to the meeting station, with me pushing on ahead to remove any twigs or stones that might trip up the great and exulted client.

Word eventually got back to my boss Calvin, who was at the time embroiled in a last ditch stand against the reprographics department in another part of the forest.

It was a fairly still day, so the sound of *'Oh fuck me, no!'* could be heard quite audibly as it drifted through the trees.

He arrived at the station a few minutes later, puffing and sweating. It was obvious he'd sprinted the half mile back to begin the smoothing of ruffled feathers.

Calvin started with the apologies and shot me a few dirty looks. I'm sure I heard him use the word *moron* at least once - and thought he probably wasn't using it to describe himself.

Discretion being the better part of valour, I removed myself from the general vicinity as quickly as possible.

A few colleagues asked me where I was going and I made up some excuse about feeling ill, buggering off before they had a chance to question me further.

I got changed out of the combat gear, surrendered my spare paint balls to the surly looking marshal and skirted the meeting station, making a bee line for the car park.

I left the site, rooster tails of mud spraying up behind the BMW alloy wheels as I made my getaway.

The groan that escaped my lips at 6.30am the following Monday morning was louder than usual. I knew full well that a chewing out of epic proportions was in the offing when I got into work.

The fat, sweaty client - thankfully - didn't remove his account from our firm, despite my best attempts to murder him in the New Forest.

He did however take to the hills as fast as his chubby feet would carry him once the job was over.

This calamity was brought down on my head because someone had suggested that it'd be good for *the morale and productivity* of the staff to spend a day shooting at each other in the woods.

Sigh.

This is what employers, team building session organisers and tanned American business entrepreneurs fail to realise: There are only one or two things that actually raise morale and productivity in the workplace.

The first of these is shorter working hours.

The second - and by far the most important - is:

Money.

Cash.

Moolah.

Reddies.

Old-fashioned sterling, guv'nor.

Forget all your well-meaning motivational posters and stupid team building exercises. Chuck out the morale-boosting *bring your child to work* and *wear jeans to work* days.

You want us to work better, work harder, work faster?

Then pay us more than the paltry amount we currently get!

…this is not the way of things, however.

Instead of paying us more money, our employers choose to spend twice as much on hiring corporate entertainers - or organising company outings to the back of beyond.

Pay peanuts and invariably… *get monkeys.*

I don't think any of us labour under the misapprehension that management are going to raise our pay unless they have to. So it's doubly important to make sure we make our work lives as pleasant as possible.

To whit, here are a few helpful suggestions:

Spalding's Top Tips For A Stress-Free Working Life

1. Never work more than the hours you're paid to do. They can't sack you for it. It's right there in your contract, alongside your job responsibilities and the warning about not stealing office equipment. If you don't have a copy then Cheryl in Personnel is only a phone-call away.

2. Don't be an arse kisser. Don't spend your time being nice to the boss and working over-time because you think it'll curry favour. It won't. It'll just make him think you're an idiot that extra work can be piled onto at a moment's notice.

3. Avoid office politics. If a colleague approaches you and starts to moan about how that bitch from Accounts got a bigger office even though he's been there longer, just smile, nod and *walk away*. You know damn well if it gets back to the bitch that you've been complaining about her, it'll be *you* she marks out for special treatment and him she'll end up shagging at the Christmas party.

4. Don't plan your future in your current job more than six months in advance. Why? Because if you start to hang all your hopes on it, it'll take on more meaning and you'll plan your life around it too much. More meaning equals more pressure, which equals more stress - and we don't want that!

5. Don't compare yourself to those around you. Just do your job and do it as best you can. Yes, Michael across the hall might have his name on the employee of the month poster, but chances are he's also got no social life, lives with his mum and can speak Klingon.

6. Get the job papers every week. Even if you're happy with what you're doing now. You never know when an amazing job will crop up and you don't want to get stuck in a rut. It can lead to depression and a feeling of being trapped. Besides, seeing that someone is advertising a job strikingly similar to yours - but for two thousand less a year - always puts a warm glow in your heart, doesn't it?

7. Try your hardest to never mention work when you're not there. It's impossible not to think about it sometimes when you're up against it, but it's vital you don't tell your friends or family what the problem is. They won't understand and you'll spend an inordinate amount of time explaining what a processing report actually is, before you get to why it's important you deliver it to the boss at 9am. Just leave well enough alone and with any luck they'll do the same.

8. Throw sickies as much as possible - unless your work involves saving lives in some way, in which case you're stuffed. Otherwise, the company isn't going to fold just because you take Monday off with an attack of the shits.

I'm a terrible one for skiving off sick.

If there's something I'd rather be doing than sitting at a desk, drinking machine coffee and eating tasteless sandwiches while I write bullshit, then a convenient phone-call to the boss to say I won't be in today is inevitable. Talking through a tea-towel into the phone always helps, I find.

I try not to do it too much in a short period of time. It's a constant balancing act. How many times can you be off ill without people thinking you're skiving?

I've got it down to about once every three months.

You also have to account for *the law of sod,* which dictates that anytime you skive off work for a couple of days to go jet ski-ing, you can be guaranteed the following week you'll get a dose of the flu and will have to go into work with it. You don't want to use up your boss's patience completely and eight days off sick in two weeks might do just that.

You know who I hate? The bloody people who get sick, but come to work anyway.

They sit and complain about how crap they feel, but also state they had to come in because they've got a mountain of work to do that just can't wait.

Bollocks.

You're not that important, you little shit.

Someone else could have handled your work load, or it could have waited until you were better!

What's more, you've now managed to spread your disease through the whole office like a modern day Typhoid Mary. We've all caught it and can look forward to a week of sneezes, coughs and headaches.

If anyone you work with comes in with the flu, cover your mouth with a damp cloth, stand at least ten feet away and threaten to beat them to death with a Kleenex box unless they turn tail and return to their sick beds at once.

To sum up: the best way to run your working life is to accept your position, never let your job take control and always remember you're there to make money.

Yes, that is a very mercenary outlook, but how many mercenaries do you know with a stomach ulcer, eh?

Good grief!

Did you hear the cracking noise my back made when I stretched?

Been sitting here for over nine hours and it's taking a toll.

Remember those noisy people outside? They're long gone now.

...everything is silent in the watches of the night. We're all alone.

If we look out of the window for long enough we might see the occasional cat crossing the street, its fur cast with a strange orange tint from the streetlights overhead. We might see the odd car - someone returning later than they'd intended from a party, or a junior doctor driving to the A&E to start a 36 hour shift.

But other than that, the world on the other side of the window is quiet.

Tranquil, you might say.

...the weather's calm tonight.

There's a slight mist hanging over the street. The kind that leaves traces of dew on your jacket when you walk through it. When you breathe out, a soft plume of cold air forms and hangs around you like a shroud.

The only sounds are from far off: the low rhythmic rumble of trains passing through the dark - and the plaintive barking of a solitary dog, missing the warmth of hearth and home.

The beast of the world is snoozing, in those magical hours between closing time and the dawn chorus.

This is when the slate is wiped clean.

When the mistakes and errors of yesterday are forgotten and the playing field is reset, ready to begin the game anew tomorrow.

It's at times like this you can *think*, when there are no interruptions and when the quiet of the night makes your mind serene.

In short... it's pretty fucking boring out there.

Puts you in mind of a bad romantic comedy - probably starring Jennifer Aniston.

Yawn.

Did you think that passage sounded atmospheric? Full of poetic description and subtle nuance?

I couldn't resist ending it on a gag though, could I?

67

It's a failing of mine. I find it very difficult to be serious, especially in the stuff I write.

I started out with the best of intentions with that passage: to write a nice descriptive few paragraphs about the world outside, only to ruin it with a gag that wasn't all that clever anyway.

The tone may have made you sleepy. After all, it is very late now.

Try and stick with me as I wind my way towards dawn though, as we've got lots more to talk about - including a nasty divorce story that's squatting at the front of my memory like a big, bug-eyed toad.

I've always been a man who likes his sleep and I'm trying to ignore the imperative to slope off to bed and go gently into that dark night.

I can hear my bed calling to me from across the hall:

'Nick... come to me Nick. Roll the duvet around you and forget the world outside.'

Evil temptress, she is.

I enjoy my sleep and yet I suffer from insomnia.

That's a fairly dreadful irony, isn't it? One that once again proves God is a practical joker - the kind that loosens the top of the pepper pot and puts cling-film over the toilet bowl.

Insomnia is one of those uniquely modern diseases that exist - at least in part - due to the lifestyles we lead.

Our old enemy the clock has his role to play in the life of the insomniac.

Having to live according to a schedule that is fundamentally alien to our mental architecture causes no end of problems.

I've laid in bed many times, knowing that the damn alarm clock is going to go off in three hours, and my brain won't shut down despite the lead weights on my eyelids.

There is nothing so exquisitely horrid than the sense of frustration you feel at this moment.

You're caught in a catch-22.

You can't sleep, which makes you frustrated and angry, but you won't be able to sleep in that mood. No matter how hard you pound the pillow or turn it over to the cool side, sleep will just not come.

There are commonly two types of insomniacs:

Those who suffer from early waking syndrome, where you can quite happily pop off to sleep at a reasonable hour, but find yourself snapping awake at four in the morning, with no chance of drifting off again.

Then there's the type I suffer from, which is delayed sleep: when no matter what you do, sleep remains a distant fantasy, until you eventually drop into an unsatisfying slumber just as the birds start to sing outside.

Sleep tends to occur in cycles of three to four hours and if you don't complete those cycles, you spend the next day walking around with sandy eyes and a grumpy demeanour.

I get insomnia when I'm stressed.

I have an overactive brain - by no means a bad thing all the time, as without it I very much doubt I could be writing this book. But there have been occasions when I'd gladly trade my imagination in for the cool empty serenity of an inactive mind that slips into sleep as easily as a hand slips into a velvet glove.

It's not like the stuff my brain occupies itself with at four in the morning is important. It would be ok if I was thinking up stunningly original ideas for books, or working out ways to make my life easier.

Instead, the silly lump of grey matter ponders such vital problems as:

'How old does someone need to be exactly to die of old age? 60? 70? 80?'

Or:

'If we didn't have bottoms, would we need chairs? Or would we stand up all the time? It'd certainly save space in trains, wouldn't it?'

Or:

'If the entire government was killed in a freak yachting accident, how long would it be until anyone noticed any difference in the way we live our day to day lives? A day? A month? A Year? Never?'

These thoughts run around my head, chasing their tails like hyperactive dogs. All the time there's a part of me screaming at them to just sod off and leave me alone, so I can get to sleep and wake up refreshed - ready to go into work the next day and apologise for shooting a fat sweaty bloke with a paintball gun.

The moment I dread more than any other is when the first bird starts to sing. I'm convinced the feathery little bastard is just waiting for me to start dropping off before commencing his twittering - letting every other bird in the area know just how tough he is.

Pretty soon they're all at it, a collection of strident high-pitched warbling, set at just the right tone to drill into my brain.

And the little gits never sing the same tune. *Oh no.*

It's always a discordant set of musical phrases overlapping one another, ending up as an incoherent jumble.

69

For the sake of variety in the orchestra, a wood pigeon starts a low monotonous hoot that wouldn't be too bad if it was timed at regular intervals. It's not though. Just as I think I've got the rhythm - a hoot every five seconds or so – he'll change to once every seven, then every two, then every ten.

Bastard!

I've tried earplugs.

They either fall out after ten minutes or prod my eardrum when I roll over on the pillow, giving me earache.

Wanking doesn't help much either.

It's supposed to leave you drained and ready for sleep, but all it tends to do is make me sweaty, cross-eyed and still *wide awake*.

Thankfully, I only go through short periods of insomnia.

Maybe a month here, a couple of months there - not a constant thing.

If it was, I'm sure I'd be locked up in an asylum by now, twitching and chasing birds around the asylum garden with a look of hatred on my face.

There are a million and one home made remedies for the condition, none of which work.

Countless over the counter medicines are available as well that seem to have equal levels of failure. These are different from the home made stuff, because they're useless *and* contain lots of horrendous chemicals that won't help you fall asleep, but will probably make your hair fall out.

Here's something I never understand about sleeping pills. Invariably, written somewhere on the box or in the instructions is this:

Do Not Operate Heavy Machinery.

What a fascinatingly redundant thing to put on a bottle of pills designed to make you fall asleep.

I can't think of anyone who's thought:

'Here I am, about to drive this enormous truck through a complicated oil refinery, where the slightest of prangs could lead to an explosion that would wipe out half of Dorset. I think I'll take a couple of Sleepy-aid pills to keep me going.'

Some of the most terrifying reading you can ever do is to scan the instructions in medicines - even the apparently harmless ones. It's enough to give anyone a heart attack as you read about possible side effects:

Nausea, vomiting, skin rashes, diarrhoea, spasms, blindness, deafness, leprosy and rickets.

…yeah, I think I'll just put up with the mild head cold actually, it sounds a much safer bet than popping aspirin into my mouth.

I even saw death described as a side-effect in something.

Death!? Death isn't a bloody side-effect!

How miserable a disease do you have to catch for death to be a more pleasant alternative?

Between the list of horrifying side-effects and the fact they don't work, I avoid sleeping remedies like the plague.

Therefore, I suffer in silence, until the period of stress and insomnia passes and a more normal sleeping routine re-asserts itself.

Without the experience of sleepless nights, I'd really be struggling by this time to write anything coherent. Lucky then that it's not too much of a trial for me to write through the night - otherwise this book would only qualify as a short story and I'd be half blind from sleep depravation by now.

Sometimes it's hard to make people appreciate the seriousness of insomnia. Explaining your condition to those who have never experienced it is a real trial. It's especially difficult when you're dealing with someone who can fall asleep at the drop of a hat and can't sympathise at all.

I've had a few conversations with people who think that I'm *overdoing it a bit* and *can't really be feeling all that bad.*

After all, it's only a few hours kip I'm missing. I'm not ill or anything, am I?

Grrrr.

My wife was always the type of person who could nod off quickly and never appreciated the misery I was in. I'll give her credit though, she never complained when I paced the floor at four am and never told me to pull myself out of it in a condescending manner.

That's the nasty thing about insomnia.

It's a psychological condition and there are some people out there who believe all such maladies are easily solved if the sufferer just *pulls up their socks and deals with the problem.*

These people need to be roasted slowly at about two hundred degrees and served with new potatoes in my opinion.

If you're lucky enough to be a sound sleeper and an insomniac crosses your path, try to be as sympathetic as possible and believe them when they say life has become a living hell. If not, you're likely to have your arm ripped out and be beaten to death with the soggy end.

Just a friendly warning.

If you're unlucky enough to be like me, then the only piece of advice I can give is to examine what's happening in your day to day life. Chances are it's having an effect on your ability to drop off and you may need to address any issues you have before the insomnia will pack its bags and leave you feeling like a human being again.

There was a client at my firm - one of the nicer ones - who ran an art gallery. He confided in me over a liquid lunch one day that he went through a period of insomnia for two years - *non-stop*.

It nearly cost him his marriage, did cost him his job and made him seek psychiatric help. He told me that every night since he has offered a small prayer to God in thanks for the uninterrupted seven hours he gets.

My admiration of the man knows no bounds.

I've been afflicted with sleeping disorders all my life. Before the insomnia came along, I used to suffer with sleep-walking when I was a boy. This isn't as bad when it comes to your well-being. After all, you may be vertical instead of horizontal, but at least you are asleep and getting some kind of rest - even if it's not exactly of a high quality.

Most of my sleep-walking activities were confined to walking around the house and bumping into the furniture. There was one occasion when - according to my mother - I thought I was Batman and she found me in the living room at four in the morning attempting to climb onto the side-board.

She said it was dreadfully disconcerting to walk in and see me hunkered down over the fruit bowl, calling her The Joker in a gruff voice and throwing Batarangs (or rather bananas) at her from my lofty perch.

You'll be pleased to know that I've been sleeping fine for the past few weeks and even the birds outside have been unable to disturb me. I'm sure they're extremely annoyed by this and are getting their revenge by crapping on my BMW.

Slurp.
Coffee. The insomniac's best friend.

I guess one reason why I've suffered insomnia in the past is because I travel a lot. There's nothing more guaranteed to muck up your body clock than changing times zones every few hours and giving yourself a good dose of jet-lag.

I still find it endlessly fascinating - and a bit weird - that I can leave Gatwick airport on a Monday morning, travel for twenty four hours and arrive in Sydney in the middle of the night the following Wednesday... or something along those lines anyway.

I've been to lots of places over the years. Sometimes on holiday with family or friends, sometimes for work - and one occasion just to get away from everything for a week on my own.

Exploring new countries, meeting new people and misinterpreting strange local customs is very entertaining.

I even enjoy the process of travelling itself, from the moment I leave my house with a heavy suitcase, to the time I walk into my air-conditioned hotel room halfway across the other side of the world - tired but happy to be somewhere where it isn't raining and overcast.

There's something very romantic about stepping out of your front door in the morning and being in another country by the time evening rolls around.

The reality is often not as much fun as the fantasy, but I'll get to that in a minute...

Even when I've been pretty skint, I've usually managed to scrape the money together for a cheap break in Europe, or a long weekend with friends in Dublin.

I'm one of those people afflicted with terribly itchy feet.

It only takes about four months of living in England before I start looking out of the nearest window, wondering what the weather's like in Quebec this time of year.

In fact, as I write this, there's a large pile of holiday brochures sitting in the corner.

73

If you get bored with our little chat, by all means take a nose through and see if you can spot any bargains.

I'm after a couple of cheap weeks in the Caribbean. If you find one, just tap me on the shoulder and show me, could you?

Thanks awfully.

Travelling isn't always fun. The romantic ideal often gives way to cold, hard reality in the blink of an eye.

Here are two very important things to remember for anyone travelling by plane in the near future:

Exit row and *bulkhead seats.*

These are the ones just behind the exit doors, or before the bulkhead on a plane. The bigger the plane, the more exit doors and the more bulkhead seats.

They are a gift from God for one very important reason: *Space.*

You're likely to get more than enough leg room if you're lucky enough to get a bulkhead seat to sit in. This will prevent you having your knees cramped for the nine hour trip to Florida you're about to embark on.

I learned the lesson of the bulkhead some years ago when I took a trip out to Las Vegas, the tackiest place on earth.

My cousin James was getting married and had decided on a stag night in the gambling capital of the world. It was designed as a blow-out of epic proportions. An entire week of drunken debauchery, scantily clad women and amateurish gambling.

James and five friends had flown out on Sunday evening direct from Gatwick to Vegas. I, on the other hand, had to fly out on Wednesday, not having enough annual leave to take the whole week off.

In my infinite wisdom, I elected to find the cheapest flight I could and chose an indirect one that would see me stopping off in the cultural Mecca of Minneapolis, Minnesota.

This turned out to be a mistake of *Herculean* proportions.

The trip started well enough.

I'd booked a taxi to take me to the airport and it arrived on time at 5.00am - when the wood pigeon was in full song. The drive was OK, with the cabbie only asking me stupid questions once every half an hour or so. He didn't get much of a reply, as I sat in the back dozing, with my head resting snugly on my flight bag.

Getting through check-in and boarding was also a smooth process, though I did have to waste a couple of hours in the shopping mall while they re-fuelled the bird.

74

I even went into The Gadget Shop on the main concourse to have a look around, which tells you how bored I was. I also had a look in Tie Rack, which really is just a shop full of ties. I have no idea how they stay in business. The world must be full of forgetful businessmen who can't dress themselves properly.

With enough time sufficiently wasted, I made a bee-line for the gate and joined the queue at security.

I did my best to not look like a drugs dealer and managed to get through with only a few suspicious glances from the customs officials.

Things went pretty smoothly from there and I wound up boarding in good time.

I hadn't heard of the magical bulkhead or exit row seat, so when I got onto the plane I found myself in a standard one, between a pleasant elderly American woman and an officious looking British man.

The plane took off and I settled back in my seat, looking forward to seeing strippers and drinking cheap American lager by the gallon.

...an hour goes by.

I start to feel the confines of my surroundings.

My knees are jammed up against the seat in front. I'm unable to put my arms on the rests because my fellow travellers have already claimed them. My bottom is starting to turn into marshmallow and my ears are getting blocked by cabin pressure.

In short, I'm not a happy bunny.

A further mind-bending hour goes by and I'm starting to climb the walls. The in-flight movie has started and it's got Jennifer Aniston in it.

The fact I've not had a cigarette in over three hours is not helping and I've only had two hours sleep in the last twenty four. There's no option for me to take a little nap here, as I've never been able to sleep on planes and was going through a period of insomnia at the time anyway.

No such problems for the friendly elderly American woman sitting next to me. One minute she's awake and laughing at Aniston, the next she's snoring like a buzz-saw. I turn to the guy on my right to share a comment about this, but he's now three chapters into a John Grisham and ignoring me completely.

Another hour goes by.

The buzz-saw becomes a chainsaw and I'm wishing I was dead.

Just when I think it couldn't get any worse, the old biddy starts to gently slide toward me.

Her head touches my shoulder and now I'm frozen in place.

I know I should politely wake her up and inform her of her invasion of my personal space - or at least give her a dig in the ribs. Unfortunately I'm British, so I sit there immobile, not wishing to be rude and wake her up from whatever pleasant dream she might be having.

I'm now in desperate need of a piss.

This presents two fundamental problems:

I have to wake up sleepy head and push past the Grisham reader.

Twenty minutes go by while I wait for an opportune moment.

I'm hoping Grisham will have to get up for a tinkle himself and I can follow him to the cubicles.

This doesn't happen.

With desperation finally overcoming my innate Britishness, I try to get up.

The American's head slithers down my shoulder until it reaches a painful angle, which brings her out of her REM filled happiness with a start.

She offers me a bleary look, turns her head and immediately goes off again.

With her safely dealt with, it's time to take on the literature fan.

Mumbling apologies, I stand up and start to edge past him, deathly afraid turbulence will kick in and I'll end up sitting in his lap. Thankfully though, I'm spared this.

I do however lose my grip on the seat in front and thump the teenager sitting there in the side of the head.

She lets out a cry of astonishment, which makes me jerk backwards and poke my arse into Grisham's face. He lets out a muffled exclamation and I swiftly move my hips forward, clouting my genitals on the back of the chair.

This makes me jerk backwards again.

Now it looks like I'm trying to hump a British Airways economy class seat.

Getting my wayward body back under control, I say sorry to both irate teen and dumbfounded Grisham reader and finish negotiating the exit from my sky-bound prison.

With both of them giving me daggers, I lope off up the aisle to the toilet, where I hurriedly shut myself off from the outside world and urinate with a bliss that's virtually indescribable.

I leave the cubicle, resigned to another six hours in the seat from Hell, when I spot three empty ones in the central section of the plane.

I couldn't have been happier to see those seats if they'd been three feet wide and had a massage unit built into them.

I gather up my belongings from the overhead compartment - trying not to look at my teenage sparring partner or Grisham - and hurry back to the three seats at speed, wanting to get there before any of the other cattle reach the same conclusion and steal them out from under me.

While the rest of the flight to Minnesota was not what I would call pleasant, at least I had the luxury of a bit of space to stretch out my legs, and didn't have the worry of mortally offending someone every time I felt the urge to take a leak.

Arriving at Minnesota was when the stupidity of getting a connecting flight became apparent.

When you've just spent nine hours on a flight with your legs cramped and your brain slowly turning to fudge, it isn't nice to know you have a further *three hours* to go before you reach your final destination.

Before even getting on the domestic flight, I had to negotiate my way around Minneapolis airport, which was gigantic. I think I'm right in saying that it covered most of the state itself and requires detailed maps to find your way around its mammoth terminals.

None of which is very helpful when you're knackered, in desperate need of a smoke and wishing you'd stayed in bed watching Desperate Housewives.

Never mind, I thought, *I'm sure if I get lost I can ask a friendly airport staff member the way.*

I did get lost. In roughly sixteen seconds.

Admittedly, I didn't help my cause by leaving the airport for a swift cigarette in the freezing cold mid-west weather outside.

Totally baffled by concourses, travelators and ill-conceived signage, I approached a security guard to ask him directions.

'Hello mate, help me out here, will you?' I said in jovial fashion.

'What'cho want?' he replied aggressively, not really living up to my idealised concept of a helpful staff member.

'Er, can you tell me how to get to Gate 43?'

'You some kind of fucking moron, pal?'

Okay, so the security guards at Minneapolis are incredibly rude, then.

Point duly noted.

I immediately saw red. I do not need a fat security guard taking a pop at me when I'm exhausted, lost and confused.

'What did you call me?' I hissed.

'A moron, pal. A goddamn moron.'

'Who the hell do you think you are, mate?'

My feathers are ruffled, my back is up and I'm ready to start swinging.

'I'm a guy who found out last night his woman is fucking another guy and is pretty damn pissed... I'm also the guy with a gun.'

He points at the black metal killing machine parked in a holster on his belt.

I'd forgotten about that.

Forgotten that in America, they'll give anyone who works in security a gun, even if they look like Charles Manson and twitch slightly when somebody mentions ethnic minorities.

It's amazing what the effect of a firearm can have on an angry temperament - when the gun is carried by the other person, that is.

My body language changes from 'irate British person in need of accurate directions' to 'terrified British person, about to start crying like a girl'.

I find myself apologising a lot in life for mistakes I make, but I've never felt saying sorry was ever as vital to my continued well-being as it was at this moment.

He cuts me off in mid-flow.

I think he realised he'd pretty much threatened an airport customer with his gun and started to back-peddle magnificently in an effort of self-preservation.

We both stand there spouting apologies - and then accepting them from one another with good grace. I even went as far as to commiserate with him on the infidelity of his partner.

I suggested he should go and have it out with her.

Without the gun, that is.

I finished by asking - very politely this time - where Gate 43 might be. He gave me a wry grin and pointed upwards.

Above us was a very large, very brightly lit sign with a huge arrow pointing up the concourse with *Gates 39-45* in very large writing beside it.

I thanked him sheepishly and wandered away, not surprised he'd thought I was a moron. I was grateful he hadn't just pulled out the gun and shot me point-blank on the understandable grounds I was an unobservant idiot.

My luck changed for the better once I'd boarded the connecting flight. I found to my astonishment and delight that the miracle of bulkhead seats had been visited on me for the first time.

It was like all my Christmases and birthdays had been rolled into one, as the stewardess led me to H8, next to the exit doors.

I couldn't believe it. It was so good I still remember the seat number to this day.

After nine hours of feeling like a battery hen, I had a seat that allowed me not only to stretch my legs out, but the chance to get up when I felt like a little stretch.

Heaven.

A supremely smug smile spread across my face and I made a point of flashing it at as many of the other passengers as I could during the flight to Vegas. I was almost sorry to leave the plane, wanting to ride my unexpected change of fortune for as long as possible.

I got out of McCarran airport quite quickly and less than an hour after touching down, I was in my hotel room with a can of beer shoved in my hand by a semi-drunk cousin James.

What happened during the actual four days I spent there is a story all its own and I'll tell you about it later.

Promise.

Twelve hours in!

Twelve hours and listen - it sounds like we've got some friends celebrating the milestone with us.

Can you hear them?

The dawn chorus has started with a vengeance and my feathered friends are heralding a new day in the only way they know how.

Thousands of birds, all basically shouting:

'This is my tree! Fuck off!'

Kind of takes the romance away when you know that, doesn't it?

Want some breakfast? I know it's probably too early and the sun's only just over the horizon, but I've got some pop-tarts in the fridge. You'll have to eat them cold, as the toaster is still knackered. It met with Spalding's towering rage after destroying a raisin crumpet I was particularly looking forward to. You can try sticking the pop tart in the George Foreman, but I'm not making any promises it'll work.

I'll just smoke another cigarette if you don't mind.

While we're on the subject of cigarettes... you might want to strap yourself in, this is likely to get a bit bumpy.

Smoking.

I *love* it.

Sorry to all you non or ex-smokers out there, but I do.

Yes, I know its bad for me and yes, I know it's expensive.

My lungs may be full of tar and my chest may wheeze like an asthmatic asbestos cleaner, but I love it anyway.

Partially, this is out of spite.

I can be a very stubborn man and when it comes to smoking, this part of my personality comes out in spades. Chances are that if smoking was still an accepted part of society no-one complained about, I would have quit years ago.

But its not, is it?

Oh no.

It seems there's nothing worse these days than pulling out a pack of ciggies and lighting one up. People look at you like you're a leper. They point and wail in disgust as you draw on your little white tube of chemical nastiness. They pompously tell you it's affecting their health through passive smoking.

Good.

Fuck 'em.

The more they moan, the more I smoke.

If people would just shut up about it and leave me be, I'd be more amenable to putting the packet back in my coat and chewing some sugar-free gum instead.

Everybody has an opinion on whether you can quit or not, like they have some divine oracle-like wisdom about your chances of kicking the habit that you're not privy to.

Just before I got married, I decided to quit - well, I thought about it anyway.

I made the mistake of talking to people about my intentions.

In idle conversation, I'd say I was thinking about quitting and how it would be nice to count on their moral support. I especially did this with my non-smoking friends. After all, they would be more than happy to usher me into their healthy ranks, surely?

Nothing could have been further from the truth.

Instead of helpful tips on how to quit, or assurances they'd be there when I needed a bit of cheering up, I got this:

'Oh, you'll never quit.'

'I bet you can't quit for long.'

Oh thanks, that's very helpful isn't it?

That really motivates me to make the grand leap into the world of patches and chewing gum.

It was the smokers around me who gave me the support I craved - pun intended. They were the ones to nod understandingly and offer words of encouragement.

Isn't that totally arse about face?

The ones you think you can count on for help put you down, and the ones you'd think would be unhelpful turn out to be your saviours.

It's a phenomenon I've never come across before.

In no other situation does it apply.

Let's use something as an analogy for it, shall we? Something that'll exemplify my point nicely:

Politics.

You are a Tory.

You've voted Tory all your adult life. You liked the way Thatcher ran things and didn't mind the fact she took away the milk break at schools. The privatisation of the country's infrastructure didn't affect you in the slightest and you even like the colour blue.

Now, over the past few months you've been thinking about not voting Tory anymore. You've been thinking about quitting the party. Giving it up.

Nothing's really been the same since Maggie left and you've just started realising how much tax you paid in the eighties.

You only have one alternative: Labour.

Sure, there are the Liberal Democrats, but if we stick to our smoking analogy, that'd be like giving up proper cigarettes to smoke those cheap herbal ones that smell like dog shit.

...no, you're right, I'd never make much of a political commentator.

Now you've made your decision, you'd like to chat to your friends to sound them out.

Applying the same attitude when discussing smoking, this is the response you'd get:

All the Labour voters would tell you not to bother trying because you'll be back voting Tory in a few months. All the Conservatives would recommend you swap allegiances immediately, because voting Labour is far better for you and puts more money in your pocket.

You see?

Crackers.

Totally gonzo, in my opinion.

Incidentally, the last passage represents the sum total of Spalding's contribution to politics within the pages of this book. I don't vote and never will, until such time as I'm presented with a political choice that is exactly that: a *choice*.

All politicians in this country bleed into one as far as I'm concerned, with any real policies buried under a mountain of spin, sound-bites and sleaze allegations. Anything funny I could say about them doesn't hold a candle to the kind of hi-jinks they seem to get into all by themselves.

Anyway, back to the point:

I'd like to say something out to all the anti-smoking organisations out there that spend millions of pounds each year trying to make us stop:

There's no point trying to educate us anymore. *We know it all.*

Every smoker is now fully aware of how bad it is, how many chemicals there are killing us slowly and how it makes us smelly and unpopular at social occasions.

You don't need to spend any more cash on heart-felt advertisements, featuring wan ex-smokers hooked up to life support machines.

The fact is, we know it's a terrible habit and if we could stop, we *would!* All you're accomplishing with your efforts is to annoy us incessantly: *'Smokers! Look how awful smoking is! Why do you do it? It's bad for you!'* We bloody *know!*

We may be smokers, but we're also free-thinking individuals who can arrive at a conclusion without you ramming it down our throats at every opportunity!

There's no point in covering our cigarette packets with terrifying warnings about lung cancer and how smoking can harm pregnancy, because we're still going to buy the bloody things anyway.

They're a drug. We're addicted. Enough said.

Why not spend the money you waste every year patronising us trying to invent a cigarette that contains no lung-killing chemicals?

Even if they did invent a miracle cigarette like that, you'd have problems convincing the government it'd be a good idea. After all, I can't see them being too pleased about all that tax they'd be missing out on.

If the ones in charge really wanted us to quit smoking, they'd ban it.

They have the power to do so and would, if the continued reliance we have on cigarettes didn't fill their coffers each and every year to the tune of millions of pounds.

There are ways that A.S.H and the rest of the cleaning living brigade can stop young people smoking in the first place. This is a far easier thing to do, provided you sell it in the right way:

Kids start smoking because it's cool. *Fact.*

It's cool because all the best celebrities do it and it shows just how rebellious and angsty you are - while you hang around outside the local One Stop, worrying old people and vandalising the bus shelter.

The trick is to take that image away.

Why not feature full page ads in the national papers of really *uncool* people having a smoke?

Gordon Brown sitting in his pants at home with a Silk Cut parked between his lips, perhaps. Or Simon Cowell lighting up a Marlboro as he tries on high waist jeans in Gap.

Or, you could start putting slogans on the cigarette packets like:

WARNING! Your parents love to smoke and will be delighted you've started too, as they will be able to nick yours when you're asleep.

Or how about:

WARNING! Smoking cigarettes will make you look like your woodwork teacher.

Trust me, these ideas will work far better than vilifying smoking to the extent that every thirteen year old in the country rushes out to buy a pack, just to show how much they're *not like you.*

For the sake of balance and to show that Spalding does have the capacity to be unbiased when the mood takes him, I also have something to say to the cigarette manufacturers:

Stop trying to pull the wool over our eyes, you greedy bastards.

You know as well as we do smoking is a hugely profitable business and will continue to be so until it's outlawed.

You know smoking is bad for us, no matter how much you try to make out it isn't.

You can stop producing low tar cigarettes, trying to claim they're better for us and are part of your effort to help smokers quit the habit. If that were true, you'd be selling them *at a cheaper price*, wouldn't you?

At least remove the high tar ones from the shelves, so we don't buy them.

But you don't do this - claiming you're trying to give people a choice.

Those little holes you're punching in the filters aren't fooling any of us you know. It just means it's harder to draw on the cigarette and more difficult to suck the nicotine out, making us more likely to spark another one up straight away to get the same hit we'd get from one regular smoke.

I've smoked since the age of eighteen, which puts me in the long term category, I guess. For nearly twenty years I've been puffing away on about ten to fifteen cigarettes a day.

I've sat there and added up all the money I've spent, and thought about all the lovely things I could have bought instead. This is always depressing and I recommend to any smokers they do not attempt it *under any circumstances.*

There are certain smokers out there who need a good, hard smack.

I'm filled with a disbelief and impotent fury whenever I talk to a *social* smoker.

I hate this lot more than the non-smokers who complain about passive smoking, or the ex-smokers who like to regale you with how easy it was for them to quit and how their sense of smell has miraculously returned.

Social smokers say things like:

'Oh, I only seem to want a cigarette when I'm out and about. Other than that, I just don't bother.'

You complete and utter bastards.

How do you do it? How do you sit there on a Saturday night, merrily chaining your way through a pack of twenty and then not have another one for two weeks? How? *How*!?

I'm not an alcoholic - rare for a writer - but I can sympathise with someone who suffers from it, when they see a half drunk glass of wine on the table at the end of the dinner party and think *how can anyone leave that? It's such a waste!*

I feel much the same way when a social smoker throws a packet of cigarettes away that still has two tabs left in it, just because it's chucking out time at the Dog and Bucket.

Comparing the two most popular drugs of choice, I loathe the double standard that exists for smokers and drinkers. Even though heavy alcohol intake seems to inevitably lead to violence and anti-social behaviour, it's still the smokers who get all the grief.

I don't understand this, I really don't.

When you weigh the two up against one another, it's plain to see that drinking is a far worse social phenomenon than smoking.

Ever hear of any small, innocent children being run over and killed because the driver was smoking a cigarette? *No.*

Ever hear of thousands of pounds of damage to property being done because a hoard of people - all smoking heavily - took to the streets in a riot? *No.*

No-one has ever got pregnant because they were smoking too heavily to remember the condom.

As far as I'm concerned, drinking is far more anti-social and destructive than smoking has ever been, so how about laying off us poor smokers for a bit, eh?

I said I loved to smoke at the top of this section, didn't I?
Lies!
All horrible, self-deluding lies!

I don't love it and if someone could wave a magic wand, making me a non-smoker instantly, I'd be happier than a pig in a very large pile of manure.

Here are a few much needed home truths to the smoking community:

Cigarettes *do not* relieve stress. They *cause* it.

Nicotine is a massive stimulant and only raises your level of tension in the long term. That calming hit you get as the nicotine pumps its way through your blood is a temporary measure, meaning you've got to spark up another cigarette, raising your blood pressure even more. It's a vicious cycle. You never relieve stress, you only relieve the craving for nicotine.

Yes, it's true you might get run over by a bus tomorrow, but the chances of it are very small, unless you're an idiot who can't obey road signs properly. The chances of getting cancer are 3 in 1.

Smoking does indeed knock five years off your life - and you may console yourselves with the fact these will be the ones at the end, but let's not forget about the pain-racked, emphysema-filled ten years that precede them.

Smoking does not make you lose weight. All it does is temporarily suppress your hunger. You'll just be *twice* as hungry once the cigarette's effect has gone and will binge eat before lighting up again - thus making you a fat bastard *and* a candidate for inoperable lung cancer.

There are a thousand and one books out there for those wishing to quit - all of which are about as useful as a chocolate tea pot.

There's only one thing that will help you quit the habit and that's will-power.

You need to resist the nicotine cravings, no matter how bad they get, and a stout door to lock yourself behind so you don't murder your loved ones in a fit of pique.

Nicotine has a half-life of two hours, which means its levels drop by half every 120 minutes. In two weeks you will have no nicotine in your body. Then it's just a psychological problem.

Spalding intends to give kicking the habit a proper go in the next few months, as he's started waking up with the kind of phlegm in the back of his throat you could hang wall-paper with, and has the lung capacity of a newborn goldfish.

What I will *not* do is mention that I'm quitting to anyone.

Neither will I buy any self-help books, nicotine patches, or ring the NHS helpline. I will however use the period of withdrawal to pretend I'm ill and skive a few days of work.

There's a silver lining in any situation if you look hard enough.

While I'm a prisoner of the evil tobacco monster, I can console myself with the fact it is my one and only addiction.

Not *much* consolation, I'll grant you, but anything's better than nothing.

Addictions come in all shapes and sizes and they don't necessarily have to be drug related.

Nymphomania may sound like a great idea we can all get behind, but as any sufferer will tell you, it's an addiction that causes more problems than it's worth. Addiction to sex isn't the kind of thing that's going to help you maintain a long-term relationship. It *is* the kind of addiction that can give you a reputation and very itchy genitals.

Robert Palmer may have waxed lyrical about how great it is to be Addicted To Love, but you try convincing the poor cow caught dogging in Sainsbury's car park at two in the morning of that.

Science-fiction.

There are people so addicted to sci-fi and fantasy they makes heroin addicts look like people with a mild interest in recreational drugs.

They have the DVDs, the books, the vast collection of action figures posed in improbable ways on every shelf in the house.

Tell them that you think Twilight is a bit childish and you're likely to get your eyes gouged out with the nearest replica pointy stake.

Don't get me wrong, there's nothing that bad about dressing up as Spock or knowing every single line of dialogue in The Empire Strikes Back, but it's an addiction nonetheless - and like any addiction, it can start to have an effect on your day to day life in ways it shouldn't.

I swear to God I once knew a lad who wore a Star Trek Starfleet costume to a funeral.

I understand how passionate people can be about their favourite TV show, but there's a time and place for everything. The burial of your great aunt Joan probably isn't it.

Mind you, I can see the priest ending his eulogy with the words *beam her up, Scotty*, as the coffin disappears in a halo of white light...

Cool.

People often develop these addictions - chemical, biological or psychological - because it lifts them beyond the drudgery of day to day life to a more exciting plateau of existence.

This is entirely understandable.

Whether you're nicely drunk in a night-club for a few hours, or curled up in front of Stargate SG1 - Series 3 Box Set, with free action figure! - for a whole weekend, you're escaping the everyday world and all its vagaries and disappointments.

Addictions can therefore be beneficial. In moderation.

The trick is to strike a happy medium.

If you're wearing gaudily coloured costumes to funerals or drunk at eight thirty in the morning - chances are you're not doing a very good job of it.

Hey!

I think I've got my second wind.

I was definitely starting to flag a bit back there, but as the sun has come up and we've marched past the fourteen hour mark, I feel a renewed sense of vigour and purpose.

I put this down to the strength of the coffee and frequency of cigarettes - doing their job as the stimulant we all know and love.

Seeing the sun come up is a wonderful thing, even if it is through a study window that hasn't been cleaned for months.

It makes you feel glad you're alive and wipes away all those strange and disturbing thoughts that roam around your head during the dark hours.

Nothing ever feels so scary in the harsh light of day and I can happily look a needle or sponge in the face with hardly any anxiety whatsoever.

Yes, yes, alright, let's deal with the sponge thing here and now, shall we?

I'm scared of them, alright?

I don't know why.

It isn't funny you know, when someone strikes up a conversation about phobias and the only thing you can contribute is that you're afraid of possibly the most harmless object on Earth.

To understand this irrational phobia more I read a very good book, which I'm going to rip-off here to fill up a paragraph or two:

Apparently, most phobias are caused by traumatic incidents in our childhood that we may forget consciously, but stay with us subconsciously for many years. These traumas manifest themselves as a phobia.

There are perfectly understandable and reasonable phobias, such as a fear of spiders, fear of heights or fear of needles.

These can be potentially threatening to life and limb and forming a phobia is partially a defence mechanism against injury or death.

I have a witty friend who as far as I know is afraid of nothing.

He likes to say the only thing he has a phobia of is thermo-global nuclear weapons, electing to go for something really big and nasty that would cause anyone to squeal in terror should they come up against the business end of one.

Of the sensible phobias, I'm only affected by needles. I hate the bloody things.

I don't care if you are administering life-saving antibiotics, you're still intent on sticking a large pointy metal object into my body, which in my book is a distinct no-no.

I'm not scared of spiders, but can understand why other people are. Black little monstrosities that skitter around the house and pop up in random places are enough to give anyone the willies.

Not liking heights is quite sensible too, seeing as the human body is ill-equipped for falling two hundred feet onto concrete.

At the other end of the phobia scale are those caused by the aforementioned childhood trauma.

The *silly* ones. These can be about anything:

Chickens, fruit, bricks, worms, top-hats, Milton Keynes, Britney Spears... anything.

In my case it just so happens to be sponges.

Don't get me wrong, put me in a room with a sponge on the table and I'm not going to start screaming in terror and bashing up the furniture to make a crucifix. But, I will start to feel ever so slightly *anxious* after a while and will be happy to leave the room - breathing a deep sigh of relief as I do.

They're just so *creepy.*

Take a look at one. It's all holes and rough textures, isn't it? You spread it apart in your hands and those holes get bigger, becoming miniature caverns leading into the heart of the monster.

Eurghh. I can't touch one. It makes me shudder just thinking about it.

Look... I'm shuddering as I write.

The irregularly shaped ones are the worst, the ones that come straight out of the ocean. All pointy and rough and ready to leap onto my face and suffocate me in seconds.

I can handle the shop bought ones. The rounded edges and tightly packed holes are a bit more bearable - but not by much.

If anyone ever plans on mugging me, they won't have to worry about finding a hand gun or a knife. All they'll have to do is wave a loofah in my general direction and I'll hand over my life-savings and first-born.

To get to the bottom of this irrational fear, I asked my mother if there were any episodes in my infancy that might account for it. She racked her brains trying to think of one, but couldn't come up with anything.

A few months later however, she remembered that when I was a small baby, I would like nothing more during a bath than to chew on whatever came nearest to hand.

My mother remembered she always had a large sponge with her at bath times and it would invariably end up in my gob at some point.

From this, I can only deduce that at some point in my mastication of the sponge I bit off a small piece and choked on it. I had obviously cleared the obstruction without my mother noticing, but the trauma had wormed its way into my subconscious, waiting to pop up in adult life and embarrass me at dinner parties.

Having some knowledge of where the problem stemmed from didn't make me less afraid of the horrid things, though.

On the contrary, I now had another thing to add to my growing catalogue of sponge-related horrors: choking to death on one.

...I've tried in the past to confront my fear without much success.

I once took a bath and had a small inoffensive sponge with me to test my mettle in the face of adversity. There it sat, on the edge of the bath, squatting like a malevolent purple, squishy monster - just waiting for me to turn my attention away for a second and launch at my head like that face-hugger thing in Alien.

Summoning up reserves of courage I didn't know I had, I picked up the sponge and started to scrub my back with it.

It felt like dragging the hand of a corpse across my flesh.

Giving one of my patented 'small girl getting her pig-tails pulled' screams, I held the offending object away from me like it was going to explode.

Then I lobbed the sponge across the bathroom.

It flew in a spinning arc, flinging droplets of water all over the shop before coming to rest with a squidgy plop down by the radiator.

The rest of the bath was conducted using a flannel, between suspicious glances over at the slimy monster, which I'm sure was leering at me.

There it stayed.

For two weeks.

I eventually picked it up with a pair of salad tongs and dumped it in the wheelie bin. Bomb disposal experts would have recognised the expression on my face as I dropped it in and slammed the lid.

That was where my great sponge experiment ended - in defeat and despondency.

For a blissful few years I managed to avoid sponges. My life was sponge free.

Then I got married.

Unlike me, my wife had no such qualms against scraping sponges across her body and would do so at every given opportunity. This meant that the bathroom became a chamber of horrors - with sponges of every shape, hue and texture lined up like malevolent goblins on the cabinet.

My mistake was not confessing I was scared of them.

It's just not the kind of thing you want to do, is it?

You've just got married and at this point your new spouse still sees you in a good light. It wouldn't do anything for your reputation to admit you're terrified of a bloody sponge.

So I suffered in silence and the sponges mounted up.

She seemed to go through them at an obscene rate of knots and every couple of months or so I'd be presented with a new one to kick start the nervous adrenaline.

I'd just about get used to the long blue sausage shaped one - enough to be in the same room with it anyway - and she'd swap the bloody thing out for some brown, plate-sized monstrosity that looked like a fungus blown up five hundred times under the microscope.

I did eventually pluck up the courage to tell her about my ridiculous phobia.

She managed to keep a straight face for nearly two whole minutes.

When I'd managed to impress upon her the seriousness of the matter, she started to sympathise a bit.

The sponges were shut away in her half of the bathroom cabinet, so I didn't have to look at them. But I always felt my heartbeat rise slightly when I opened my half to get the shaving foam out.

...I'm going to move on now, as I've given myself the creeps.

My phobia may be pretty extreme and most of the more garden variety ones - creepy crawlies, being trapped in close spaces, etc - are perfectly understandable.

The twenty first century has given rise to a lot of phobias that didn't exist a hundred years ago.

They revolve around things unique to the last few decades.

Fear of in-flight meals or hospital waiting lists, for instance...

The most prevalent phobia that's appeared in the last forty years or so is technophobia.

A large number of people exist to whom the thought of having to programme the Sky Plus box in order to record House for the next six weeks is terrifying.

And what do the technology companies of the world do, just as we do get used to something? They go and make the bloody things obsolete, that's what!

Instead of VCRs and CD Players, we're now faced with black, slim-line MP3 Players and blu-ray recorders - and we're back at square one.

The manufacturers may claim they're simple and easy to use at the touch of a button, but that still doesn't change the fact you have to *find* the bloody button on the remote control in the first place.

Luckily for me, I've been able to grasp recording TV shows to hard disk with relative ease.

The same can't be said for computers.

I don't know how they work *at all*.

All I know is you switch it on, wait a couple of minutes while it sorts itself out, hum along to the Windows theme as your desktop pops into view - and download porn for seven hours.

When it comes to the complicated inner workings of the machine or the complexities of software packages, I'm at a total loss.

I use a computer station at work, but I'm limited to using word processing packages, and never delve into the murky world of Adobe Photoshop or Microsoft Excel.

My knowledge certainly doesn't extend to fixing problems when they inevitably crop up.

Every time the machine so much as looks like it might be thinking of locking up, I'm on the phone to computer services faster than you can say *this program has performed an illegal operation and will shut down.*

I've got no idea what to do when computers rebel against their human masters and start going hay-wire.

Yes, I can sit at this desk and type a book out in Microsoft Word quite happily.

I guarantee you one thing though, if it freezes and the blue screen of death appears in front of me, I will scream, thrash around on the floor and curse the day some nerd in California invented the microchip.

It's no wonder so many people are frightened of using computers.

All of them - along with a huge amount of other electronic equipment - are linked to the internet and many other vast, rumbling PCs across the planet.

Because of this, there's a scary tendency to think that at some point you might press the wrong button and shut down the Japanese National Grid.

There's a woman at work who can't for the life of her work out how to send e-mails properly. Outlook Express makes her palms sweaty and her head pound.

She makes a real effort with it anyway, and for the most part manages to use it with a degree of success.

She did once accidentally send an e-mail to everyone in the company - some two hundred and fifty people - telling us all in great detail how she was going to buy a crotchless thong from Ann Summers, which she hoped would *get him hard for the first time in months.*

It transpired the e-mail should only have gone to her best friend, though I doubt her husband would have been happy with the fact his wife was telling even one person about his impotency, let alone two hundred and fifty.

As a man who'd once crapped himself in public, I could relate to her embarrassment.

Fear of phones.

There's another uniquely modern phobia.

To some poor folk, the phone sits in the hallway like a coiled snake, ready to strike - or in our handbags or jacket pockets, now mobile telephony has become a way of life.

How many times does your phone ring and its bad news on the other end? I bet it outweighs the good calls by a hefty percentage.

Never mind that, what about the cold calls that come through just when you've settled into a nice bath, or are trying to do something constructive like write a book?

They're an annoying little addition to modern life aren't they?

Double-glazing, car insurance, home insurance, special offers and low interest loans - which sound like a good idea, until you realise you'll still be paying the interest off ten years after you've died.

I had a call from a loan company a few weeks ago.

Not only was it supremely bad timing - the shark documentary had just got to a really gory bit - but it came from a guy with an Indian accent so thick I could only understand one in every ten words:

Ring ring. Ring ring.
Me: 'Hello'
Him: 'Is dis meester Nicharlas Spilding?'
Me: 'What?'
Him: 'Is dis meester Nicharlas Spilding?'
Me: (pause to digest) 'Yes. Can I help you?'
Him: 'I'm calling frum Quick-Loans tventy fur hoor, zir.'
Me: 'What?'
Him: 'Quick-Loans tventy fur hoor, zir. I am calling from dem.'
Me: (Catching on) 'No, I don't want a loan, thank you.'
Him: 'Wait! Wait! I am not zelling loans! Honestly, zir. I just wunt to speek to you about an ovver zat is not a loan, zir.'
Me: (curious, despite better judgement) 'Alright, go on then.'

Him: '...Rite now, Quick-Loans tventy fur hoor are offering loans at cheep cheep rates, zir!'

Click.

Give me a break.

Cold calls aren't the only problem.

The automated phone menus are a hellish experience. You only want to ask the guy at the bank what they're opening times are and yet you have to spend three quarters of an hour punching in numbers seemingly at random, only to reach your intended destination and find an engaged tone at the other end.

Aaargh!

Now they've made it even worse by having voice recognition.

This means you now stand in your hallway shouting numbers and words into the phone like a mental patient:

'One!' (wait)
'One!' (wait some more)
'Three!' (keep waiting)
'Two!' (pick nose)
'Saturday!' (wait)
'Yes!' (wait)
'Four!' (lose temper when it cuts out and you have to start again).

It's enough to make anyone want to give up and go and live on a mountain... one equipped with a dedicated Wi-Fi router and proxy firewall.

Technophobia is virtually unavoidable when you think about it.

The more reliant we are on machines and the more we entrust the running of our lives to them, the more risk we're taking that they'll break down and pitch us back into the stone age.

I find this a far more believable vision of an apocalyptic future than you'll get in movies like The Terminator or The Matrix.

These films would have us believe that the machines will become so smart that they'll usurp us as the dominant species.

To me, this shows rather a disproportionate amount of faith in the reliability of computers.

In reality, before they'd got as far as subjugating the masses, they'd probably suffer a hardware conflict and start making quacking noises.

I think being catapulted back to the stone age is far scarier.

This Human Race Has Performed An Illegal Operation And Will Shut Down.

You may have noticed that there isn't a phone in this study. This is deliberate.

There's nothing like a cold call from Mr. Patel in Calcutta to put you off your creative stride.

I tend to like it as quiet and peaceful as possible when I write. That's why you won't find a radio in here either, be it on the desk or in a pen.

It's also no accident I'm writing the majority of this book on a Sunday, when it's nice and quiet.

Well, supposed to be anyway.

The rather strange man who lives next door has just started mowing his lawn. The tinny buzzing noise you can hear is the ancient lawnmower he uses to cut around the begonias.

And no, I don't know why he's wearing a sombrero either. It clashes with the bright blue shorts and orange tank top he's wearing, I know that much.

Okay.

Now it's daylight and we've livened up a bit, let's get into the whole business of my failed marriage.

It isn't going to be pretty, I assure you.

Maybe I should include one of those warnings like you see on movie posters:

Warning: The following chapter contains scenes that may be unsuitable for small children and newly-weds.

My wife's name was Sophie - a name I still think is beautiful, despite the slings and arrows of our marriage.

Look... I'm using the word *was* as if she's passed away. She hasn't, it's just easier than writing *ex-wife*, something I'll never like doing as long as I live.

Let me lead you down the long path of memory to the time when I first met her:

Here we are then, standing in a popular high street electronics shop.

———

97

That's me, leaning on the camera display with a vacant expression on my face. It's getting on for five thirty in the afternoon and we haven't had a customer for nearly an hour, so I'm passing the time thinking up new and exciting ways to avoid sponges.

Don't look like a happy boy, do I?

Not surprising really.

I'm now twenty five and find myself in a position that I didn't plan on when I was eighteen. By now I'd completed my degree and was entertaining plans of starting a career in journalism.

Therefore, it came as a huge shock to find myself working as a trainee assistant manager in Currys.

The reason for this is annoyingly prosaic: I need money.

I was as poor as the church mouse's less solvent brother when I left university and had to take the first job that came along.

Well, that's a lie.

I actually spent the first year after my degree pompously telling everyone that normal work was beneath a person of my talent and I wouldn't get a job until it was one that suited my unspeakable talents.

This notion was soon kicked out of my head when I ran out of savings, ran up a huge overdraft and had to move back into my parent's house.

So along comes the job at Currys.

The pay is low and the hours are long, but it gives me enough money to stave off the wolves and pay the rent.

It's also an easy job.

I spend my entire day telling customers just how great the ten times optical zoom on that Kodak is, or explaining the finer points of Sky to the slightly confused pensioners standing in front of me looking like a deer caught in the headlights of an oncoming truck.

The guy I work with most of the time is a genial sort of bloke called Adam.

Adam is also a university graduate, who has inexplicably found himself working as the manager of an electrical shop, despite being assured by his careers advisor that a job as an architect would be a guaranteed dead-cert once he'd graduated.

We have quite a lot in common.

He's not afraid of sponges but can't stand chickens. We both like a nice cold beer to go with our cigarettes and enjoy a good porno as much as the next man. He loves BMWs, and spends a great deal of time telling me how great they are and how I should buy one as soon as I can afford it. He's never crapped himself in public, but has thrown up over a policeman, which is pretty bad in itself.

—

A firm friendship builds over a few months and as we reach the day my wife walks into my life for the first time, I'm happy to have found a mate on my wavelength.

…Adam is currently sitting over there at the counter, playing patience on the computer and puffing his cheeks out periodically in the time-honoured gesture of boredom.

Is the scene set firmly in your mind?

Good. Then let's bring in the star.

I'm turning to walk over to Adam, curious as to whether he's beaten his computer opponent yet, when a girl walks into the store and my life changes.

She's beautiful…

She's graceful…

She has *big tits*.

Her hair is a deep shade of brunette and swings behind her back in a glorious cascade of body and vitality… you can tell I write marketing copy, can't you?

She has large, luminous eyes and a soft expression that in no way betrays the steel she's got running down her spine.

Her nose is a tiny bit on the large side, but fits into the rest of her face well enough not to notice most of the time.

She's wearing jeans and a t-shirt - tight enough to let me notice those boobs - and wears them in that effortless way some women have of dressing scruffy, but looking like a million dollars at the same time.

I register all this in the couple of seconds it takes her to walk into the shop.

My senses have become heightened and my heart has started to beat a little faster. A smile spreads across my face as she nears and I start to think of a witty and friendly thing to say that'll put her at ease.

The smile drops off my face faster than the trim on a French car when she changes direction and makes a bee-line for Adam, who is now investigating the contents of his left ear hole with a prospecting finger.

Oh fabulous, I think.

The first attractive woman I've seen in months and she's going over to chat to Adam - who in my opinion is far less handsome than me and doesn't deserves the attention of such a fine looking woman.

As she approaches him, a grin spreads across Adam's face and I find myself fantasising about scooping his eyes out with a rusty spoon. I've gone from a state of boredom to nervous excitement and into rampant jealousy all in the space of thirty seconds.

Then Adam says something that makes me glad to be alive:

'Hi, sis!'

Sis?

Sister!

She's his sister! Fantastic!

My mood takes an upswing immediately - then dips again when I realise that all the time I've known Adam he hasn't mentioned being related to this lovely creature once.

Why not?

Why have I never met her before?

Has he been keeping me away from her?

Maybe he's one of those protective brothers who police their sister's relationships with a ruthlessness that'd make any Gestapo officer proud.

...or maybe she's already taken and he's been trying to spare me the misery of being in the vicinity of such a goddess, knowing I can never have her.

Then, she speaks:

'Alright, toss-face. I see you're working hard again.'

'Yep. What have you been up to? Selling your body to the local perverts outside Tesco again?'

How dare he!

How dare he insult this beauty in such a way!

My attitude has of course been coloured by my burgeoning desire and I've forgotten that one man's ideal woman is another's annoying little sister - who deserves a Chinese burn at every opportunity.

Instead of being mortally offended by her brother's comment, Sophie gives him a vicious rabbit punch to the upper arm and pokes her tongue out.

I'm in love.

I don't have time to change into a nice suit. I don't have time to comb my hair and gargle with mouth wash. I don't have time to rehearse a suitable chat up line.

I do have time to take a deep breath and compose myself, before sauntering over and interrupting their conversation.

Sophie looks round as I approach.

Adam, being a man and knowing of such things, sees the way my demeanour has changed and gives me a speculative grin, leaning back in his chair to watch proceedings unfold with a delighted and expectant look on his face.

This is a ritual he's seen a few times and enjoys it every time.

I can only take it as a good sign that he hasn't taken one look at me, started shaking his head and sketching the sign of the cross. Must mean his sister isn't entirely unapproachable.

'Hello,' I say.

'Hello', she says back.

The following conversation was one that took place on two levels, where the subtext was totally different from what's being verbalised, like so:

'I didn't know Adam had a sister.'
Translation: I'm delighted Adam has a sister and I've automatically got a leg up on all the other men that have tried it on with you because he's my mate.

'Yeah. He's a pain in neck, but sometimes he's alright.'
Translation: OK, sonny boy. I've got your number. You're thinking just because your mate is my brother, it'll give you swift access to my underpants. Don't count your bloody chickens. However, you're not bad looking so I'm happy to engage in a conversation with you, for the time being at least.

'He's never mentioned you before. What's your name?'
Translation: Your brother is in fact a complete bastard and I will be having words with him about neglecting to introduce us. What's your name? Please don't let it be Nora, Enid or Helga.

'Sophie. Yours?'
Translation: You're not doing badly so far, sport. Keep it up and who knows what'll happen.

'My name's Nick. Nice to see somebody got the looks in your family, this ugly bastard here certainly didn't.'
Translation: Yes, I've just paid you a massive compliment. I would like to insert my penis in you at the nearest opportunity. Furthermore, I'm showing you how close my relationship is with your brother with some good natured insults, as this might improve my chances.

'Fuck off, dickhead,' Adam tells me.
Translation: I'm loving every second of this. Unlike you Spalding, I'm totally at ease right now and am thoroughly entertained by your efforts to pull my little sister. You're my mate and I'd be pleased to see you going out with her, but keep the details to yourself please. Oh, and if you hurt her, I'll rip your spine out.

'Thanks very much. He is an ugly little troll, isn't he?' says Sophie.

Translation: Yes, I like you. Congratulations. You've got over the first hurdle and haven't come across like a complete wanker. I'm happy with the way things are going and my first impression is favourable. I'm looking forward to the second stage of negotiations. My pants are staying on for the minute though pal, I'm not easy.

The conversation went on for about fifteen minutes.

It turned out Sophie had come in to tell Adam that their mum wanted him to call her about his doctor's appointment last week - meeting a guy was the last thing on her mind.

This is usually the case when bumping into your future partner.

You can be guaranteed that all the time you're desperately searching for miss or mister right, they'll never happen across your path. But the second all thoughts of love and communion are out of your head: there they'll be, opening up a whole new world of possibilities.

Sophie turns to leave the store, administering a friendly poke to her brother and a winning smile at me as she does so. And yes, she does look back round as she walks out of the shop.

Excellent.

Nothing has passed between us that would suggest the foundations of a love affair or anything. I haven't asked her out on a date or declared my undying love. But I like to think some groundwork has been laid and the next time we meet, I'll have the chance to really get stuck in and charm her properly.

Once she's gone I start to interrogate Adam.

To begin with, I fake an air of casual interest, but by the time he starts to give me the kind of answers I want to hear, my true feelings have come out.

Adam's replies to my searching questions go something like this:

'She's twenty four Nick... She works in a florist Nick... Yes, she's single Nick... No, I don't know if she's happy being that way Nick... No, I don't know if she'd like it if you asked her out Nick, but you're welcome to give it a go... She's been away in Scotland with our dad for the past few months Nick, that's why you've never met her... No, I'm sure she didn't meet anyone up there, she would have told me Nick... I'm seeing her at the weekend Nick... Yes, I'll ask her what she thought of you when I do Nick.'

The poor bloke was getting more and more cheesed-off with the bombardment of questions and was no doubt relieved when the end of the day came.

When I got into work, I had no idea I'd be in love nine hours later.

That's how it works, isn't it?

Love doesn't account for the clock, or schedules or calendars. It doesn't care what you're doing with your life or what plans you may have. It waits for you, like a lion in the high grass waits for a passing antelope.

And like a lion, love looks soft and beautiful - but has *claws*.

It took three weeks to see Sophie again and the time went by painfully slowly.

Adam saw her and did his duty as a friend by letting her know I was interested - something she no doubt realised herself anyway. He then did his duty as a brother by letting me know her positive - if guarded - reaction.

Eventually, he manufactured a night down the pub with his girlfriend and invited both of us along.

The evening went astronomically well.

I was dressed in dashing casual gear. I felt good. I smelt good. I remained virtually sober throughout the whole thing, not wanting to ruin my chances with any stupid drink related cock-ups.

Sophie and I got on like a house on fire.

We talked about work, university, my ambitions to be a writer. At some point Adam and his girlfriend made their excuses and Sophie and I continued to chat until closing time.

It was *wonderful*.

I drove her home, as any honourable knight-in-shining-armour would, and she favoured me with a gentle kiss on the cheek when I saw her inside.

We planned to meet up again at the cinema, and I drove home at roughly four hundred feet above the tarmac.

The movie we went to see was Saving Private Ryan - her choice.

I put my arm around her as she cried softly during the harrowing parts.

After the film, we spent an hour in the nearby pub discussing the war and its aftermath. She's deeply affected by the film and so am I.

It takes us about three months to fall in love completely.

They are the happiest months of my life.

Still are.

They tend to be for everyone, don't they?

The feeling you've at last met someone who *fits* is indescribable.

True love is never about need.

Need is a greedy little emotion and never leads to anything good.

True love is about *want*.

You *want* to be with this person, you feel comfortable around this person, you know that they complete you.

True love is mutual. It puts you at ease and gives you the confidence to tackle any problem head on.

True love makes you *stand.*

And that's how it was for me, as my relationship with Sophie deepened into something more than just another one to add to the list.

I knew after only a few weeks that this relationship was going to be long-term and it didn't bother me in the slightest. I was ready for some serious commitment - much to my surprise.

As we got to know each other better, we fell in love even more and those months flew by faster than I could believe.

One year goes by and we start to plan for marriage.

We only managed to hold off that long because we're both fairly practical people and wanted to make sure we worked as a couple before taking the plunge.

In hindsight it was pointless to wait. I think we wanted to be married after only a few weeks of being together.

It pays to be patient sometimes, though.

Her job at the florist pays well, and my job at Currys has increased in salary to the point where I'm feeling good about the financial future.

We decide on a small ceremony in a church we'd once had a picnic in. It's in a small village, about ten miles away from the city.

We invite thirty close friends and family. It's slightly overcast on the day, but it doesn't spoil things in the slightest. The wedding goes off without a hitch and we all get nicely drunk at the reception.

Sophie and I make love that night in the hotel, and while it's not the most rampant or earth-shattering sex we've ever had - no body oil, karma sutra positions or handcuffs - it's the most memorable by far.

After the wedding and subsequent honeymoon in Jamaica (bulkhead seats on the plane) we return home and start house hunting.

This ain't much fun at all.

You'll recall that I'm crap when it comes to buying large things, and as houses are about the biggest thing you can buy, the levels of my inadequacy sky rocket. In the face of viewings, estate agents reports and mortgage arrangements I collapse under the weight of my own neuroses.

This is the first time Sophie's skills at negotiating come to the fore. Which is just as well. God knows what kind of dive I would have bought otherwise.

Case in point:

We looked at a house in a leafy country lane, set in a picturesque village - the same one as the church where we had the wedding. On first inspection, the place looked great and I was deeply enamoured with it.

I'm an idealist and when I see something that fits my ideal, I tend to act first, ask questions later. That was certainly the case with this house. It looked beautiful - with climbing ivy on the walls and a spacious front garden, perfect for miniature gnomes.

After only inspecting the outside of the house, I was ready to buy it and move in yesterday.

Sophie counselled caution and suggested it might be a good idea if we saw the inside of the place first.

This was an *extremely* good suggestion.

Seen the Texas Chainsaw Massacre?

If you have, you'll have an idea of the interior of this house. If you haven't, just imagine dirt, dust, a disturbing *meaty* smell and a lot of nasty detritus on the floor.

Rotten furniture, musty carpets, broken glass, and what looked like the bones of at least two or three small animals were just some of the delights to be found in this chamber of horrors.

This really was a house built in the country: smelly, dirty and covered in pig-shit.

The estate agent who showed us round admitted it could do with *a bit of a clean up*. This was like saying that Osama Bin Laden could do with *a bit of a telling off*.

We leave the house on Nightmare Avenue, returning to my flat for a good hot shower - and never speak of the place again.

Incidentally, I had cause to drive along that leafy country lane a couple of years ago and saw that the roof had fallen in.

There was a sign saying *abandoned* on it. I might have substituted that for one that read *Abandon All Hope, Ye Who Enter Here* - having been inside.

Bearing this near disaster in mind, I let Sophie take more of the lead in deciding which houses to view from then on.

It took us a couple of months to find the right one, but when we do, we find a place we both love.

She loves it because it sits in a quiet street. I love it because there's a spare room big enough for me to convert into a study.

We move in - Adam helps out a lot by nicking the Currys delivery van for the weekend - and settle into the kind of domestic bliss most people hear about, but never experience.

All is well in the house of Spalding and his Mrs.

I don't mention the thing with the sponges for several months.

Sounds fantastic, doesn't it?
And it was.

It was great through the first four years of our marriage. It continued to be great through Sophie's pregnancy, the birth of our son Tom - named after her grandfather - and my change in job from Curry's assistant manager to marketing copywriter.

We had tiffs, obviously. Caused by one petty thing or another - including expensive BMWs - but for the most part, they were small and easily settled with a few gentle words of apology and the odd bunch of flowers from the petrol station forecourt.

So where does it all go wrong?

How does the marriage of Nicholas and Sophie Spalding end?

Did I cheat on her?

Did she cheat on me?

Nope.

Nothing so easy to identify and pin down as the cause.

What is it that destroys this particular nuclear family?

Time, my friend: *Time*.

It's rearing its ugly ahead again, as it has several times in this book. But on this occasion, it's not a minor annoyance or an unavoidable element of modern life we can ruefully make jokes about.

This time, it's *serious*.

Lack of time becomes the real problem. Lack of quality time with one another.

Not planned, not expected and certainly not wanted - time drives a rift into our wedded life.

It doesn't happen at once. Its effects are slow and insidious.

Eight years pass before things come to a head.

I'm working hard by this time - very hard indeed.

I'm spending more and more time at the office, getting in earlier and leaving later. I get home at gone seven o'clock most nights, sometimes only catching a brief few minutes with Tom before he goes to sleep. I then spend an exhausted hour on the couch with Sophie before turning in, getting up again in the morning and repeating the whole cycle.

I can safely say in the average day I see my wife for maybe a total of two hours if I'm very lucky. Sometimes it's as little as one and never more than four.

The situation is exacerbated by her job at the florists, which keeps her busy from early morning until early evening in a schedule as hectic as mine. Even when she is home, she's on the phone to a supplier or client, as I sit on the couch watching Sky News, trying to keep my eyes open.

Our poor son sees more of the expensive nanny we've had to hire than either of his parents. I wouldn't have felt quite so bad, but I'm sure the woman's moustache is starting to frighten him terribly.

Things gets worse.

Sophie and I start to argue.

Properly, this time.

She accuses me of thinking work is more important than my family. I accuse her of much the same thing. It doesn't occur to either of us we're both in the same situation and should work together, instead of throwing recriminations about. *Practise what you preach* is a maxim never employed in our household.

To cut a long - and rather painful - story short, it reaches the point where we're not sleeping in the same bed and barely speaking.

Something has got to give.

It does in spectacular style one cold January evening, when we have an argument of epic proportions that wakes Tom from his sleep and probably sets off car alarms down the road.

She tells me she's leaving me. I tell her that's fine by me.

...I never think she will, of course, I'm just angry as Hell at that moment.

Anger turns to astonishment and grief as I realise she's going to make good on the threat.

Two weeks later, Sophie has taken Tom and moved in with Adam and his wife.

I will at this point give Sophie a huge amount of credit for establishing with her family that the split was as much her fault as it was mine. I tried to do the same when explaining things to my relatives.

I think this went a long way in making the break-up easier.

There's nothing guaranteed to make a separation harder than if the families of those involved end up throwing insults at each other across the battlefield.

When I try phoning Sophie at her brother's house, Adam does his best in the awkward position he's in and tries to get her to come to the phone. Sophie won't - which in hindsight is understandable.

We both got on each other's nerves so much by this point that any conversation was bound to end in another barnstormer of an argument - something neither of us needed.

I hoped against hope this would be just a temporary measure and we would smooth things over enough to salvage our marriage.

My hopes were in vain.

While we were apart physically, we grew even further apart emotionally. Unlike many break-ups, this emotional parting of the ways was a mutual thing.

Living without Sophie became easier as time went by and I became very aware of the fact that I was rapidly falling out of love with her.

This scared and disappointed me in equal measure. I just couldn't believe that the strong love I felt for her had slowly bled away over a period of eight years and it was equally hard for me to accept the same thing had happened for her.

But, there it was.

Undeniable and true. No matter how much agonising I did over it, it wasn't going to change.

If I started to miss my wife less and less, I started to miss my son more and more.

Ever since the day he'd emerged squalling and covered in yucky stuff that doesn't bear mentioning, Tom had become one of the central focuses of my existence.

I'd gone from seeing him every day to only seeing him once a week.

Sophie understood how much I loved him and was happy to let us spend time together whenever I wanted to.

I get down on my knees and thank God for the person Sophie is.

I hear so much about messy divorces and bad break-ups from friends and colleagues that I'm eternally grateful for the way mine went.

We may be apart and only linked by our son, but I still - and always will - respect and love Sophie for the understanding and maturity she showed during that difficult time.

It would have been very easy for her to become selfish and unreasonable when we split - thousands of people do - but she didn't. It's because of this I've watched my son grow up and been allowed to be a father.

The divorce proceedings started about four months after Sophie moved in with her brother. Just like our courtship, it went smoothly and was over with a minimum of fuss. Sophie was happy for me to keep the house and I was happy to pay her as large an amount as I could for child support and welfare.

I may moan about my job more than is sometimes necessary - and it may have contributed to our divorce - but it's always kept me solvent enough to provide for my son, which makes it just about the best job in the world, don't you think?

Sophie and Tom now live about six miles away in a very nice flat, large enough for both of them. I visit Tom regularly and have him to stay with me as much as possible.

When I do visit her house, Sophie is always welcoming and we find ourselves talking like civilised adults. Sometimes one of us will remember something humorous that happened in our time together and we'll recount it. We'll have a good laugh over our cups of coffee while Tom plays in the sandpit I bought for him for Christmas.

Sophie told me about a month ago that she's started seeing a guy who works for the floristry supplier she uses. I couldn't be happier for her.

Adam and I still meet up now and again for a pint and he even tried pairing me off with the area-manager from the Currys store where he still works. I thought she was uglier than a bull dog chewing a thistle - and told him so.

I'm single at the moment and am fairly happy to be that way.

I do however have my eye on a rather nice young lady who works as a P.A for a marketing client.

She has blonde hair - and when I think about it, bears something of a resemblance to a certain university student I embarrassed myself in front of many years ago.

Do I regret my marriage to Sophie? Not one bit of it.

Do I regret that our marriage ended because of that clock on the wall and how it reminds us of all the time we lose and can never get back again?

Every single day.

It could have been worse and it could have been better.

On the whole, I'm satisfied with the memories I have and the time we spent together. The best were when the clock on the wall was forgotten and the love we shared made time stop completely.

Phew. Dark stuff, eh?

Look - even the sky has clouded over a bit in sympathy.

That chapter changed the tone of the book and maybe left you feeling a bit melancholy.

Maybe it's because of what you read, or maybe you're just remembering a time in your life when love came knocking and ran off again just as quick.

Better to have loved and lost, I guess...

Best we move on and get to something a little more cheery. That'll get rid of these unwanted feelings of sadness, and put a smile back on our faces.

Spalding will now consult his internal warehouse of ideas, recollections and musings in an effort to accomplish this:

Give me a minute.

It's very dusty back here and the shelves go on forever.

I must get some new lighting as well - that fluorescent strip overhead is totally inadequate, especially the way it keeps flickering like that.

Dum de dum.

Bear with me, I'll find something in a mo...

A-ha!

This will do nicely:

Death.

No, no, bear with me on this, it sounds better than you think.

Who says death can't be funny in the right circumstances?

It's all about the context.

Picture this:

Spalding is at a funeral. Not normally what you'd call a laugh riot of an occasion, but in this case it's true. The person being sent on their final journey is a great uncle of mine.

His name was Gerald and five days ago he suffered a massive coronary that shuffled him off this mortal coil in double quick time.

I hated Gerald.

Everybody hated Gerald.

He was the kind of mean spirited human being who only exists to take up valuable oxygen and make the lives of everyone around him a bloody misery.

He would make a point of puncturing all footballs that had the temerity to end up in his back garden. The kids who'd inadvertently kicked the ball over the fence would come to the door and ask him if they could have it back.

Some would be polite, some wouldn't. It didn't matter to Gerald. They all received the same answer of *'Fuck off, you little sod'*, no matter how polite they were.

He would take great glee in stabbing the ball with a handy pair of garden shears and then throw it back over the fence a couple of hours later for the kids to discover the next morning on their way to school.

He also once hit a thirteen year old boy in the head with his walking stick, because the lad had thrown a water bomb at Gerald's front room window. Lovely, eh?

The man was also a massive racist.

Not in a humorous, politically incorrect kind of way, but in a deeply disturbing fashion that made you feel sick.

To him, anyone who wasn't white - and preferably British - was somehow sub-human. Every black person was a *stupid nig-nog* and every Indian a *dirty pakkie*. He belonged to the BNP. He might as well have been a card carrying member of the neo-Nazis.

I never received a Christmas present from him once.

Nor did anyone else in the family, despite the fact he would brag as loudly as possible whenever he had the chance about the vast sum of money he'd accrued over the years, through *wise investment and canny saving*.

His wife, who had the strength of character to stay married to this ogre for forty years, eventually had an affair with one of the gentlemen at her tango class and gratefully fled the nest.

Gerald burned everything of hers she'd left behind and started telling his friends how much of a slut she'd been. He'd also tell of how he would regularly have to give her a slap to keep her in line.

'Good riddance,' he said and I'm sure he meant it.

Gerald had been a soldier for twenty five years. During that time he'd never fired a shot and always managed to squirm his way out of any difficult assignments. He stole thousands of pounds of equipment while working as a supply co-ordinator at the barracks and snitched on everyone in his platoon he didn't like.

A real peach of a human being and an utter coward, I'm sure you'd agree.

He was hated by all with equal measure. Even the people he liked to think were his friends shuddered every time he walked into the pub.

And please don't think this was the type of man who couldn't let his emotions show, protecting his inner-child with a cold exterior. A man who was only looking for a bit of help, love and support to bring out the Samaritan within...

He wasn't.

He once shot a cat dead with an air rifle, because it had made the grievous error of walking innocently across his lawn.

He was, in fact, a cunt of the highest order - and that will be the only time I'll use that word in this book. I wouldn't have used it here, but no other word can truly encapsulate my feelings for Gerald.

You'd think that nobody would want to go anywhere near such a man's funeral. That no-one would be interested in celebrating the life - and mourning the passing of - a man who once ordered his wife to abort the baby he'd planted in her womb because *I ain't having no kid fuck up my life and take all my money*.

In actual fact, the funeral was packed to the rafters.

When Gerald died, the person elected in his will to execute his final wishes was my absent minded uncle Sid.

The rest of the will was naturally as mean-spirited as the man who'd written it and nearly all of Gerald's accumulated wealth - which I heard was around the two hundred thousand pound mark - was essentially given to his investment brokers.

He had however ear-marked a few thousand for his own funeral expenses.

In a spectacular display of bad judgement, he's nominated Sid to arrange this grand event, but hadn't bothered to lay out how he wanted the money spent. I guess in his cruel little mind, he harboured the fantasy that his family would want a lavish ceremony that would see him interred in grand style, in a mausoleum Stalin would have been envious of.

He obviously thought Sid would carry out his wishes in a way Gerald would have found appropriate.

This didn't happen.

Sid may be absent-minded, but he was also a massive practical joker, who suddenly found himself with several thousand pounds to blow on a funeral for someone everyone despised and was glad to see in the ground.

Sid had *plans*.

He had plans to make sure Gerald got sent off in a style appropriate to the way people felt about the old bastard.

We all received invites to the funeral.

They had a picture of Hitler on them.

A speech bubble extended from Hitler's mouth that said:

'Ve vould like to invite you to the ze funeral of Gerald, ze zecond most evil man of ze twentieth century'.

Gerald was to be buried, not in a huge mausoleum standing in the shadows of a huge cathedral, but in a tiny graveyard in a much smaller, grottier church, just off the motorway, near the local recreational ground.

Drug addicts would go there to shoot-up on a regular basis.

I think the police were slightly perturbed when Sid went into the station one day to ask them which cemetery had the most criminal damage done to it in the area.

It was apparent that Sid had spent as little as possible on the funeral itself and as much as possible on the refreshments to be drunk before and after. The local off licence hadn't seen so much business since the Queen's Jubilee.

The invite - printed on very cheap paper - said we were to meet at Sid's place, where he'd bought a large gazebo with some of the proceeds and stuck it in the garden. There we were supposed to get drunk before wending our way to church.

Friends and family - along with anyone else Sid had fancied inviting to the party - turned up and much drink was imbibed in the two hours before the funeral. Sid warned us not to get too plastered, as he wanted us to enjoy the festivities he'd planned at the service properly.

At the church we sat in the pews, with Gerald shoved in a plain pine coffin at the front. It was completely unadorned and there were no wreaths or messages of condolence anywhere in sight.

The vicar of the church - who probably thought we were all mad and dreadfully unkind - delivered a brief sermon. It was standard stuff about how God loves us all and how glorious it will be when we've snuffed it and get to sit by his side in Heaven all day, playing ping-pong and polishing our haloes.

When the vicar was done, Sid got up and started his eulogy:

'Dearly beloved, we are gathered here to see Gerald Shearwater buried… and not a moment too soon.'

This was greeted with laughter, some of it a bit guilty.

'Gerald has gone to be with God now and will be in Heaven as long as it takes the almighty to work out what a bastard he is… and transfer him down to Hell on the next passing goblin.'

More laughter. We're starting to warm up now.

Sid continued with the eulogy, making passing references to Gerald's horrendous personality, terrible body odour and gut-wrenching ugliness of body and spirit.

Now we're laughing *quite a lot.*

It's not so much what Sid is saying, but the deeply serious, heart-felt tone he's employing that makes the whole thing funny. The man has impeccable comic timing and knows how to work a crowd.

He finishes the eulogy with the words:

' ...and now, we will bow our heads, while a suitable hymn is played, that will see Gerald on his way to the pearly gates. Pray silence for this most revered piece of music.'

Sid bows his head. We follow suit.

What blares out from the church's antiquated sound system is this song:

Ding-Dong The Witch Is Dead from The Wizard Of Oz.

Now Gerald may not have been a witch. Hell, he wasn't even female, but the sentiment is entirely appropriate.

That's it for me...

As soon as I hear the strident high-pitched singing of munchkins and fairies, I'm off to the races.

Laughing like a tree full of monkeys on nitrous oxide, tears roll down my face and snot dribbles from my nose. I'm pretty drunk by this time as well, making me laugh even harder.

Laughter is infectious as well all know. And the infection spread like wild fire as Ding-Dong really gets going.

Some people held it together enough to start singing along and it was the first time in history a bunch of laughing goons stood wailing: 'Ding-dong, the witch is dead, which old witch? The wicked witch!' in a place usually reserved for solemn prayers and sonorous hymns.

By the time the song finished, nearly everyone was in drunken hysterics. Sid was unable to continue and announced the service was officially over.

We filed out of the church, wiping our eyes and noses, stumbling out into the overcast afternoon - even the weather hated Gerald.

A few stayed to see the old bastard unceremoniously dumped into the ground and then wound their way back to Sid's place, where the party got into full swing. Free booze was on offer to all, along with a vast array of tasty treats Sid has spent the rest of the funeral cash on.

The blow-out went on into the night and by midnight I was approaching the bowel loosening stage, so decided to catch a cab home.

I've had better nights out than that one, but not by much.

You may be offended at the idea of a large group of people taking the death of one man as a cue to have fun and party. I can only say that if you are, you need to remember the *context*.

Gerald was very unpleasant.

I've given you a few examples of how nasty he was, but it would take a whole book to catalogue all of them.

Never was a more fitting tribute given to a more deserving individual.

There may be some offended, not so much by how we treated Gerald, but by the way we seemingly trod all over the traditions of the church. To these people my response would be: *Lighten up.*

Religion can be a strong and guiding force in a person's life, but it can also make mountains out of molehills with great ease.

There are many religions in our world. All different, but all essentially doing the same job of making us feel better about our own mortality.

No matter if you're Christian, Catholic, Muslim, Hindu or Buddhist, you turn to religion to seek some comfort and solace against the spectre of death that's the one true constant in the universe.

Everything dies.

It's a scary concept, isn't it?

So we try to make the inevitability of death more palatable with religion.

Ironic then, that the one thing in human history that's caused more death and blood-shed than anything else *is* religion. Countries and races have spent centuries - and a lot of money - trying to destroy anyone who doesn't agree with their religious standpoint. And the practical upshot of all this? Lots of corpses and divides between faiths so wide you can't see the other side.

If you have a mind, try hunting down some summaries of organised religions and do a bit of comparing and contrasting. You'll find that other than the names, places and dates, every religion is essentially saying the same damn thing:

'Love your fellow man, have faith in the infinite, create life and don't destroy it.'

There you go, Spalding has boiled down millions of words of Holy Scripture and thousands of sermons into one convenient sentence.

Think I'm oversimplifying the issue?

I don't. Not for a *second.*

Sadly, the human race can't seem to grasp the concept that we're all barking about the same thing, and we continue to kill one other in ever-increasingly despicable ways. Anyone engaged in killing or oppression in the name of their religion is a fool - too stupid to actually read what their holy books are trying to tell them.

If someone gets their knickers in a twist about people being disrespectful at the funeral of man nobody liked, they should take a long hard look at the people who are devout, and use it as an excuse to kill.

That's *far* more disrespectful, don't you reckon?

I've always considered agnosticism the right way to go.

Not a religion, more of a state of mind.

Its tenant is that none of us have a hope in Hades of knowing the true nature of God, so it's best to hold our own council, keep an open mind and stay out of the way when the religious lunatics come to town.

It also means that when we do die, we can stand in front of whatever form God may take, happy in the knowledge we never said anything bad about him - or her.

...well, nothing bad enough to warrant a trip to Hell on the next passing goblin to join Satan and his new chief lieutenant Gerald Shearwater.

I think Gerald was an atheist, in actual fact - which could explain a lot. Atheists are generally very grumpy and surly individuals, who you wouldn't invite to the family barbecue.

I kind of wish Gerald had been Buddhist, because then he would have been re-incarnated as a slug, and I could have taken great joy in pouring salt on him.

I like the idea of re-incarnation.

Don't believe a word of it, but like the concept nonetheless.

There's something amusingly ironic about returning as a lower form of life and having to deal with all the pollution and rubbish you produced when you were human and thinking you were the bees knees of carbon-based life forms.

What's the order you'd progress up the food chain if you were re-incarnated?

Slug – chicken – dog – lion – dolphin – football supporter – human being?

If so, I'd be quite happy to call a halt to the process as a dolphin.

I think I'd thoroughly enjoy a life messing around in the ocean, doing tricks for the poor, dumb human beings.

When I do die, I have - in my infinite wisdom - decided that I want to be shot out of a cannon into my grave, while a chorus of singers dressed as nuns belt out It's Hip To Be Square by Huey Lewis And The News.

I figure if your death can't be heroic or meaningful, then it might as well be entertaining.

It's mid-afternoon and time is starting to run low, methinks.

I plan on bringing an end to this before midnight tonight, so it only leaves me ten hours to finish.

I can get a few more chapters in before we take our leave of one another and return to the real world though, no problem.

By this time on a Sunday, most of those chores are usually done.

The car is washed, the dog is walked and the Sunday papers have been read from cover to cover - the lifestyle section and funny pages anyway, no-one actually reads the financial section, do they?

As the day moves along, thoughts turn to eating roast dinners and watching TV as the old girl on the Antiques Roadshow looks pole-axed when told the snuffbox she found in the attic during the last clean out is worth twenty grand.

Sunday is the day we traditionally commune with God, if we happen to follow a faith that holds Sunday as the day of worship.

Fitting then, that I just spent most of a chapter slagging off organised religion.

I'll probably be struck by lightning any minute.

Religion isn't the only way we try to cheat death's hold on us.

If there's one pursuit we take part in - and enjoy a lot more than praying if we're honest - in order to poke the grim reaper in the eye, its procreation.

We do this to ensure the survival of our name and heredity, if not our actual physical being.

I'll get on to the business of children and how we raise them in the next section (see? I am thinking ahead now and again). For the moment though, let's discuss the fun bit that comes before:

Sex.

Great, isn't it?

The one thing we can truly thank God for above anything else is the gift of a good, hard fuck.

He could have been nasty and decided the best way for humans to create new life was shaking hands or head-butting each other. Instead he made the process a great deal more enjoyable - and if we're lucky, very sweaty.

Because he made sex such an enjoyable thing, a great deal of it conducted across the planet is purely recreational.

The purpose of making the beast with two backs may be to create babies and keep the human race on its feet, but that often takes a big back seat to covering each other with chocolate and hanging from complicated looking leather contraptions.

There may be stories in this book that may have made you feel a touch of sympathy for old Nickle-Pickle, but I'm here to tell you not to worry.

Yes, I've had my fair share of humiliation and angst, but there's one thing that's always raised my spirits and kept me on an even keel. One thing I can always look to for comfort and solace.

You really shouldn't concern yourself about me too much because:

I have a large penis.

See?

Everything's not so bad, after all.

Not that I'm bragging. No, no, no.

It had nothing to do with me that God looked down on my moment of conception and said in a big, booming voice:

'Spalding shalt have a big wang'.

Thus it was done, and lo... Spalding's father did celebrate and walk about the cities and the streets, proclaiming to the heavens how proud he was of his offspring's meat and two veg.

You may cast your mind back to the story about Callie and how I lacked the confidence to chat up the blonde minx with the button nose.

You may be thinking: *'If he's got a big schlong, surely he'd have no problems chatting up women?'*

Unfortunately, it doesn't work like that.

If it was socially acceptable to whop the bald-headed champ out on the first meeting and wave it around to show your virility and strength, then yes, I would have had a lot more confidence. The kind you could bounce rocks off.

Sadly it isn't and I had to fall back on charm, which was virtually non-existent due to fear of rejection and a skinful of lager.

There might be women in this world who'd respond favourably to this chat-up line:

'Nine inches, love. Nine inches.'

…but if there are, I've never met one and would probably be terrified if I did.

It's only on the occasions I've managed to get past the first few dates - like with Sophie, for instance - that the girth of my manhood has started to pay dividends.

At university, if I could have created a reputation with the ladies as a three-legged man, it would have made pulling a lot easier. The problem was, I already had a reputation as the guy who shits himself at parties.

My penis could have been two feet long and able to move like an elephant's trunk and it wouldn't have mattered much.

Having a large penis is cool, but in no way makes you a good lover. Nobody is good in bed when they start out and I was no exception – cock like a donkey's not withstanding.

My first sexual encounter was definitely not one for the books.

The girl in question would probably agree if she ever reads this.

Her name was Annabelle. Annabelle Itchen.

Fantastic name, eh?

Ripe with piss-taking potential, that one. I'll leave you to think up some suitably humorous variations. God knows how the girl must have suffered during her school years.

By the time I met her, Annabelle was eighteen - as was I - and we were going to the same college.

College isn't like university, as you still tend to hang around in the same old groups you did at school, but spend less time outside the Co-op worrying old people and vandalising bus shelters.

College exists in that awkward time between trying to fit in at school with everyone else - and making every effort to be an individual once you get to university or into a job. It's kind of like floating around in limbo for a couple of years, working out who the hell you actually are.

Annabelle had moved down from London and was a bit of an outsider. This was fine because I was too.

I never really bonded much with friends at school, as I kind of liked pensioners and found bus shelters to be largely inoffensive.

I went to a large city comprehensive, where I rubbed shoulders with the petty criminals and McDonalds staff of tomorrow, so didn't have much in common with anyone, being a nerdy little sod who liked Star Trek and sandwiches with no crusts.

Annabelle was in the same English Literature class at college, so we had something to talk about in the student common room. We got on well and I was pleased this made some of the other lads jealous.

While Annabelle wasn't a glamour model in waiting, she was an attractive lass with auburn hair and a winsome smile.

I'm not going to recount how we got together, as I've already covered meeting women and establishing a relationship elsewhere. Suffice to say we fancied each other and started going out immediately. It was all pretty run-of-the-mill and probably similar to your own experiences with first love.

After a month of kissing and awkward fondling, I was ready to take the plunge into full-on copulation.

Thankfully, so was she.

We arranged a special evening at her parent's house, while they were off sunning themselves on the continent and completely oblivious to their daughter's forthcoming deflowerment.

I went round on Saturday evening, condom stuck firmly in wallet, half filled with excitement about finally losing my virginity and half terrified of getting it wrong and poking my dick in her ear hole.

For men, virginity is the exact opposite of money: You want to lose it as quickly as possible and don't care when it's gone.

For women, virginity is *just like* money: They don't mind giving it away, but would like to spend it on something worthwhile that they won't want a refund for once the dust has settled.

I would have been more than happy to get down to business the moment she opened the front door, but Annabelle had other ideas.

She'd planned a romantic meal.

She'd put the lights in the lounge on a dim setting to try to give it an atmosphere of romance and banished the family dog to the spare bedroom, not wanting it to intrude on our night of passion.

The meal was a Kentucky Fried Chicken Fat Bucket and the lounge lighting made me slightly myopic, but it's the thought that counts.

We chatted as we ate. The kind of conversation two people have when the same thing looms large in their minds, but don't want to bring it up for fear of jinxing everything.

After the meal, we sat down on the couch and put the telly on. Raiders Of The Lost Ark was on BBC One and my desire to deflower young Annabelle was temporarily put out of my head by whip-cracking archaeologists and spooky religious artefacts.

When the film ended, I remembered why I was there and put my arm around Annabelle, making the first move.

My heart pounded like a jack-hammer and she looked like somebody in front of a firing squad.

We continued as best we could and eventually started to relax into things.

We kissed. I let my hands wander over her shirt and she did the same over my face and neck.

There was a brief pause when in her excitement, she poked me in the eye and I had to spend five minutes blinking away tears, while she apologised and went to get some tissues.

Service was resumed and I thought it best to divest her of her clothing before she poked me in the other eye and I was rendered unable to because of blindness.

Her shirt came off with no trouble.

I spent a few moments ogling her breasts in adolescent awe, before starting on the bra.

Ah, the *bra*...

A contraption of such fiendish intricacy, it has baffled men for decades.

It looks so simple:

Undo hooks and remove.

Nowhere near as complicated as a computer or Sky Plus box.

So why are some men - including me at this point - unable to get the damn thing off inside five minutes without a copious amount of swearing?

Having a hard-on the size of Northampton and hands shaking like a shaved polar bear doesn't help much either.

Annabelle willingly sits forward in a cramped position while I fumble around swearing, before she takes over and whips the hooks open in a nano-second. Thanking her profusely, I try to pull the bra off in teenage excitement.

She's not ready for this and the bra nearly garrottes her when I yank it up instead of forward, as is the customary procedure.

This time it's me apologising as she sits holding her throat making gagging noises, with her head between her legs.

Deciding further undressing is best left to the experts, Annabelle and I strip independently of one another.

Standing in the lounge's dim lighting, we both peer at each other through the gloom.

I definitely like what I see. She seems to feel the same way and gives me a good look up and down. Her eyes widen perceptibly when her gaze reaches my purple headed love truncheon.

...yes, you're right. Half the reason I decided to tell this story was so I could use all the comedy nick-names for male genitalia I could think of.

There we are, butt naked and drinking in the sight of one other.

We come into each others arms and now the extraneous clothing is out the way, it's a lot easier to get at all the interesting, soft bits.

Now, I could get pornographic here...

I could spend the next couple of paragraphs going on about throbbing members, heaving breasts, milky white thighs and bodily fluids that are hell to shift in the wash.

I could, but then this book will only be bought be a certain clientele who like to wear large coats, dribble slightly and have furtive expressions.

Therefore I will skip the gory details.

…try to not look so disappointed.

To be honest, most of what transpires is awkward, nervous and tentative, so it wouldn't make much of an erotic story anyway.

There's another pause while I put on the condom I'd been carrying in my wallet for over a year. The pause is lengthened considerably because I try to put it on the wrong way round, nearly causing myself a night in casualty.

I yank and pull for a few moments, getting slightly worried at the alarming shade of red little Spalding has gone, before realising my error and swapping the condom around for another try.

If we both hadn't been very nervous teenagers embarking on our first sexual experience, we could have laughed off most of these mistakes and carried on regardless.

But as we *were* very nervous teenagers, each cock-up was greeted with a lot of silence, followed by comments like *'are you ready to carry on?'*, *'you'll have to move round a bit,'* and *'aaargh! wrong hole!'*.

Would it surprise you to learn I had an orgasm and Annabelle didn't?

No, I thought not.

I'm sure she was very pleased to gaze up into my eyes, with her legs locked round me for dear life and watch me grimace like a lunatic as I finished up.

I'm sure it filled her with delight to hear me let out the groan of a dying elephant and collapse on top of her, spent and sweaty.

And I'm positive it made her night complete when the family dog - mentioned briefly at the top of this anecdote - wandered into the room and started to bark at the top of its lungs.

It wasn't a big dog. A collie I think.

But at that moment it looked like a ferocious monster, ready to rip out my throat for daring to insert my penis into one of its owners.

The bloody thing must've managed to open the bedroom door upstairs with its cunning canine intelligence, responding to the sounds of grunting and moaning it heard downstairs.

Being the archetypal protective hound, it must have thought something dreadful was happening to Annabelle and had decided to come to her rescue as any faithful pet would.

It looked really, *really* fucking angry.

Seeing and hearing the dog, I went from 'limp and sexually exhausted' to 'terrified and bolt-upright' in the space of a second.

It'll go for my cock! I thought and hastily covered my rapidly shrinking manhood.

Annabelle started to shout at the dog, telling it to calm down. Maddie - as it was called - refused to do this and continued to threaten me with loud barking and gnashing teeth.

Annabelle leapt to her feet as naked as the day she was born, and grabbed her loving pet around the scruff of the neck, pulling it away from me.

By this time, I've managed to secure some form of protection with one of the cushions from the sofa.

I slam it in front of my genitals, not caring that if a dog with a set of sharp teeth really wants to bite my todger off, then a small lilac cushion from Ikea isn't going to stop it. Nevertheless, it made me feel better.

Annabelle succeeded in herding the raging mutt out of the lounge and up the stairs, locking it back in the bedroom.

As she got back to the lounge, I'm wrestling with my jeans, while at the same time offering up prayers of thanks that the naked girl had saved me from a nasty canine mauling.

I have to say my behaviour for the rest of the evening was not on top form. I hung around for another hour or so, but then started looking at my watch every thirty seconds, chucking glances toward the front door.

'Do you want to go home?' Annabelle said.

Yes I did.

With my virginity gone to the winds and my nerves shattered by the diabolical doggie, I wanted nothing more than to show the evening my heels and get back home for some serious sleep. No insomnia or superhero related sleep-walking in Spalding's life at this point.

I gave Annabelle a half-hearted kiss at the door and wended my merry way home, pleased to not be a virgin anymore and relieved to still be in possession of the organ I'd accomplished it with.

My attitude to Annabelle was very poor that evening and if I had the chance to apologise to her now, I would.

We saw each other a few more times after that night and the sex got a little better - we made sure there were no domesticated animals about for one thing - but the relationship spluttered out in a couple of months, as so many teenage romances do.

A lot of people say their first sexual experience wasn't great, that it wasn't that exciting. I have to agree with the first point, but on the subject of excitement, I can't think of anything more pulse-pounding than the prospect of having your winkie-woo bitten off by an incensed collie dog.

As life has gone on, I've got better at screwing, and I enjoy it immensely.

Even when actual sex isn't on the cards, I have to confess that the odd *gentleman's entertainment* film has made its way into my DVD player.

There's nothing wrong with a bit of pornography in my book.

Where I do get a bit uncomfortable is when pornography becomes a group activity - conducted in public.

Yuck.

It should be a purely solo venture, behind closed doors, with the curtains shut!

I've never had the desire to see a skin flick in a cinema and my one brush with public *sex-capades* is one I'd rather forget.

Cast your mind back a few chapters and you may recall I talked about a trip to Las Vegas with my cousin.

I promised I would speak more on the subject and the time has arrived to do just that.

As Vegas is generally considered to be the home of sinners and dodgy morality, what better place to investigate the idea of watching sex in public, eh?

James had one ambition while in Las Vegas. He wanted to visit a strip club.

Not just any strip club, but one where young ladies would entertain the customers with large and vibrating rubber implements.

It may sound like James was a colossal pervert, but in reality he just wanted to broaden his horizons before marriage.

Personally, I would have broadened my horizons by not marrying the pasty looking rodent of a woman he was betrothed to, but then who am I to judge?

So off we all went one night, seven partially drunk British men in a cab, wallets stuffed with bills of low denomination for the g-strings of the local good time girls.

The cab driver, a grumpy looking individual who'd done this kind of thing a million times, takes us to a strip club called Rhinestones.

This turns out to be a dreadfully tacky looking place - even by Vegas standards - with some large plastic cow-girl statues parked outside the entrance and the kind of exterior lighting you'd normally find on an aircraft carrier.

It may have been one o'clock in the morning, but I still needed sunglasses to look at the damn place.

We all go in, naughty school boy expressions on our faces, and are greeted, not by a semi-clad lovely, but by a grinning fat man in a suit three sizes too small for him.

'Hello boys! Come for some fun with the girls, have you?'

No mate, we're here to check your plumbing...

James, too carried away to bother with sarcasm, nods his head enthusiastically, requests a private table and *the works*.

The fat pimp grins even more and leads us to a private booth at the back of the club.

We walk past gyrating ladies on four separate stages. They're being eye-balled by a variety of truckers, tourists and all-American college boys. The way they sit: heads up and bodies forward like penguins at feeding time, is a trifle unsettling.

Disconcertingly, as we are led past the tables and chairs I notice that under the ultra-violet lighting there are white stains all over the seats.

Now I don't know what these stains are. They could be beer, they could be spirits. But I've seen enough forensic crime shows on the TV to think they could be something much nastier.

I'm now starting to think this trip is a bad idea.

Trying to put it out of my mind, I sit down in our private booth - cut off from the rest of the club with a lovely set of bright orange curtains - and await developments.

The fat guy takes our money and retires.

A few moments later, three women enter the booth.

They are not what you'd call stunners.

Stunted maybe, but definitely not the kind of woman you see frequenting the front cover of glossy men's magazines.

None of them look particularly healthy and I'm pretty sure the tall brunette is in her late forties.

The red head in the cowboy hat looks like she's suffering with a good case of acne and the blonde one appears to be cross-eyed.

They're dressed in a variety of sexually alluring outfits, which feature a lot of leather, rubber and - of course - rhinestones.

Two of them jump onto the table in front of us, while the cross-eyed one walks uncertainly over to the back of the room and picks up a large black bag. I'm fairly sure she's walking slowly so she doesn't bump into any of the walls.

James and the others start to make strange cat calls and grunts of excitement.

When an American man does this it sounds loud, brash and heartfelt. When a British man does it, it sounds very awkward and like he needs the toilet.

I join in, trying to get into the spirit of things. I'm not doing a very good job, as my mind keeps returning to the horrible stains I saw out front.

The two girls start to fondle one another on the table. Items of clothing are removed, and much slapping of flesh and licking of lips follows. The cross-eyed one starts to delve into the black bag, producing an increasingly eclectic variety of sex toys:

There are long ones, there are short ones. Some vibrate, some are tied together with rope.

They come in various shades of black, red, purple, pink and green.

One looks like something you'd clean your fish tank with.

Cross-eyes hands these to the two on the table, who proceed to insert them into various orifices.

Contrary to what you might believe, this is *not* arousing.

It's just... *mechanical*.

I might as well be watching robots putting a BMW together for the sexual thrill it's giving me. You can easily tell these girls have done it a thousand times for groups of men much like ours.

You get the impression that while they're poking implements into each other and moaning gratuitously, they're also thinking about what food to buy for the cat and what time Oprah's on that evening.

Unbelievably, I'm starting to get bored.

The others look more into it than I am, though I'm sure they're faking most of their excitement to keep up appearances.

Miss Cross-eyes asks me if I'd like her to sit in my lap. I give her a terrified look and metaphorically straighten my tie.

I'm acting so damnably British, it almost hurts:

'Oh... er... no thank you. I'm quite alright as I am, but you're very kind for asking.'

What a stud, eh?

She looks at me in disgust and turns to help with the implement insertion.

This gynaecological display goes on for another five minutes, with the girls collecting up a nice bundle of singles, fives and tens.

By this time, I've started looking closely at the orange curtains, wondering if they'd look good in my bathroom back home.

The fat guy puts an end to the fun by sticking his head through the curtain and telling us the show's over. I'm quite relieved to hear it.

The girls immediately stop acting like rutting hyenas and bugger off back into the dressing room to clean up before the next load of horny idiots come-a-knockin'.

I ask James if he's happy. He nods his head slowly, as if not entirely sure he believes it.

We return as wiser men to the nightclub proper and proceed to get drunk on vastly over-priced lager.

I certainly drink enough to be able to sit on one of the bar stools without worrying about what fluids have dried on it.

As we leave the club to return to the hotel, I can't help looking at the plastic cow-girls out front and thinking that there really isn't a lot of difference between them and the ones inside.

Not the most titillating or exciting of trips in the end, despite what the brochure may have advertised.

I guess I'm just not one of those men who can get aroused by sexual displays in public - where intimacy is non-existent and the time it lasts is directly related to how much cash you've got in your wallet.

For me, sex has to involve a level of interest from *both* parties - otherwise the thrill is most definitely gone.

James got successfully married to his woman and as far as I know the Vegas sex show has never been mentioned in their household.

Every time I see him, I like to go cross-eyed for a moment and ask him if he's cleaned his fish tank recently.

It always cracks him up.

That ended up being a long chapter didn't it? Sex is always fun to talk about.

Mind you, the theory might be good, but the practical is *way* better.

We're closing in on the magic twenty four hour mark now. I've kept a few milestones in my head while writing this and passing a full day is definitely one of the big ones.

I may have a beer to celebrate.

You can have one too if you like. It's one of those low alcohol ones that claims to taste exactly the same but never actually does.

That's good marketing for you:

Ten percent truth, seventy percent bullshit, twenty percent cleavage.

Twenty four hours ago I was down the park with my son Tom.

...it seems like months ago now, not just yesterday.

Funny how that can happen when you miss a night's sleep.

Tom likes the park, mainly because it gives him a chance to run around on those sturdy little legs of his, with no danger of head-butting any nearby obstacles such as walls, sofas or other people.

I'm fascinated by the way he makes the simple task of crossing a playing field into an action-packed adventure.

I think I envy him as well.

It must be wonderful to still live in a world where nothing is mundane and everything you see is a potential plaything.

He's at that age (five) where he's got the sense to appreciate the wonder of the world around him, but hasn't had the magic of life knocked out of him yet by cold, hard experience.

Can you remember being like that?

If you can, you're luckier than I am.

I meet people from time to time who are *always* smiling and drift through life with a happy go lucky attitude that means they worry less, stress less and live in the moment.

I'm convinced this is because they still remember what it was like to be that dreamy five year old, running across an open field, giggling at things only they can see.

I love my kid without reservation and without condition.

131

Yes, sometimes he can be naughty. He can be wilfully disobedient and will push the envelope of parental patience as far as it can go.

But he has this way of diffusing your towering rage after he's put pen marks all over the new sofa:

As you're about to give him a telling off of epic proportions, he'll give you a slight, but winning smile. You try to ignore it as much as possible and keep on track.

Slowly though, the smile will start to work its magic and you find yourself trying desperately not to copy it.

The words coming out of your mouth may be *'That's very naughty, Tom'*, but the impact is ruined by the smile traitorously spreading across your face.

He'll smile even more - and *you'll* smile even more.

He'll then start to laugh and so will you.

And when you're giggling with him, you'll decide its best to give up on the scolding and instead you'll stumble into the kitchen, laughing for a few more minutes before realising you've just been neatly handled by a five year old boy - who's gone back to drawing all over the sofa.

I find that both amusing and *deeply* troubling.

Like many men, I was thoroughly unprepared for fatherhood.

I never liked children and would throw menacing glances at the two brats wailing in the corner of the restaurant, their caterwauling ruining my chicken jalfrezi and pilau rice.

Squalling bags of mucus was the way I'd describe babies, and indeed when Tom was born, he *was* a squalling bag of mucus.

But he was *my* squalling bag of mucus and that made all the difference in the world.

Sophie told me she was pregnant as I was eating a bowl of spaghetti hoops.

I didn't spit them out in comedic fashion, but did sit there staring at the spoon for a few seconds.

I remember speaking to her from roughly ten thousand miles away:

'Really? How far along are you?'
'Two months. You'll be a dad before the summer.'
'B-b-baby.'
'Yes, that's right Nick. I'm having a baby.'
'F-f-father.'
'Yes, that's right Nick. You're going to be a father.'
'S-s-spaghetti.'
'Yes, that's right, Nick. You're eating a bowl of spaghetti.'

When I recovered from the shock, I was pleased to find I was happy about the whole thing.

Sophie was happy too. She put back all the sponges in the bathroom cabinet she had been planning to attack me with had I not been so enthused.

Neither of us are very patient people and don't like surprises, so the first order of business was to find out what sex the baby was.

I was extraordinarily pleased it was boy.

I would have loved a girl equally I'm sure, but was glad that I wouldn't be pulling my hair out in fourteen years, as she went out on her first date with the local teenage scumbag.

In the next seven months we attended to all the tasks future parents have to. We bought books, which we barely read because they were universally pompous, about the business of raising a child. They irritated both of us beyond measure.

We picked out a cot and redecorated the spare room. I wanted it covered with pictures of ninjas and soldiers for my brand new bouncing baby boy. Sophie wanted it a nice neutral lilac.

She won.

We bought lots of baby equipment. It all went in the downstairs cupboard and I had to shift my car magazines into the loft.

Grrrr.

We went to classes for new parents, where Sophie learned a lot and I thought up some lovely new stories while I daydreamed and paid absolutely no attention to what was going on.

She got bigger and I tried not to make fun of the pronounced waddle she developed in the final stages.

I know women are supposed to *glow* and look healthy when heavily pregnant, but my wife was more inclined to scowl and look angry - mainly at me.

We talked to parents with babies, who all gave us their sage advice about how to handle the birth. Sophie and I both thought they were smug gits. We promised each other we wouldn't turn into them once Tom was born and kept that promise for a whole two weeks after he popped out.

Tom's birth was quick.

Sophie was only in labour for four hours and out came Tom: healthy, noisy and messy.

Very messy.

No-one prepared me for just how messy the experience would be.

Sophie wanted me in the delivery room as Tom came into this world and who was I to argue? She was the one going through the agony, and the least I could do was to be there to suffer the insults and death threats she'd want to throw my way.

The death threats were mercifully absent by the time we got to the final stages, as Sophie was spending too much time breathing like a malfunctioning steam engine to do much more than throw me a few angry glances.

She'd also had an epidural, which took a distinct edge off her towering rage. This was good for both my eardrums and the bones in my right hand.

I knew the birthing process was not like it is in the movies.

The baby does *not* slide out like it's on a greased ramp and is not a gleaming shade of pink, with a few small blood spots on its head. It does not cry for a couple of seconds before settling down into a soft cooing noise - and the mother does not take her new born child in her arms and look lovingly into its eyes.

What actually happens is that the baby arrives into this world covered in some of the weirdest looking shit you've ever seen outside the latest horror movie.

It doesn't slide out, but emerges incredibly slowly from its home of nine months, eventually plopping out with an unpleasant squelching noise that wouldn't sound pleasant in Dolby 6.1.

It's covered head to toe in horrible gunk and its head has gone lumpy.

It's extremely pissed off and lets you know this by immediately launching into a blatting scream that rattles your eardrums and makes you wish you'd brought earplugs.

The child's mother is *not* bathed in a rosy afterglow either, but is covered in sweat, eyes goggling out of her head. Her hair is plastered to her face and her skin is a disturbing combination of hectic red and pallid blue. It looks like she's gone twelve rounds with Mike Tyson at his most anti-social.

And *then* comes the horror of the afterbirth.

As much as I carry the lovely memory of my son entering this world with me at all times, it is irrevocably linked with the memory of seeing that placental sac sliding out of my wife like a harbinger of the apocalypse.

I could tell you all about it, but if you're a woman you'll already know - and if you're a man, I wouldn't want to spoil the glorious moment for you when you do eventually become a dad. Wouldn't want to spoil it for you *at all*.

...yes, the face I'm making now is evil, isn't it?

I didn't faint during all of this, I'm very proud to say.

I looked away, *yes*.

I looked back and wished I hadn't, *certainly*.

I felt nauseous and had to hide the look of horror on my face, so Sophie wouldn't hate me for the rest of eternity.

Childbirth isn't pleasant...

134

If it's supposed to be a miracle, then I'll take my chances without anymore in this lifetime, thanks.

It features elements you don't want to know about if you haven't been through it. Suffice to say that I've talked about bodily waste already in this book and won't bring it up again here.

Yuck.

Tom did not stop crying and make cooing noises as he sampled his first few minutes of life. He continued to cry, making it quite plain to all those in attendance that he was *not fucking happy* with being woken up and squeezed unceremoniously from the safety of the womb into the cold, harsh light of day.

The nearest I can get to that feeling must be when you struggle awake from a disturbed night's sleep, knowing you have to get up and go to work - multiplied by a million.

I'd also like to think that when he came into the world, some part of him recognised the clock on the delivery room wall, knew the significance it would have in the next sixty-five years of life - and screamed with all his might.

He continued to wail as they wiped him down and wrapped him in a blanket, ready for depositing into the arms of his parents.

I was fascinated by the mechanical way the hospital staff did this.

It was such a huge event in my life, I fully expected everyone around me to act like it was too:

'This is the birth of my son!' I wanted to scream. *'He is more important than any other child! Treat him as such!'*

But instead of viewing my boy as the second coming, the delivery staff went about their business in a methodical and professional way which I found very disappointing. I wasn't expecting them to start a close harmony rendition of the Hallelujah Chorus, but a bit of joyous weeping and genuflection couldn't hurt, surely?

Sophie took the baby in her arms once the doctor had decided he was healthy. This appeared to involve laying him on a table, poking him a bit, shining a torch into his orifices and squinting thoughtfully.

Sophie held the boy close and - miracle of miracles - Tom did start to quiet down as his mother rocked him back and forth.

There's a moment when the enormity of it hits you.

For me, it was looking down at my son as he stared back with an expression of stunned confusion.

At that moment, I accepted that my life was going to be completely different from that moment on. I now had a responsibility to care for my son and make sure he was always safe and loved.

The little bastard still looked like Winston Churchill though, and didn't do anything more constructive than cry and chuck mucus everywhere.

Sorry, but there it is…

I'm not going to sit here and wax lyrical about how beautiful new born babies are, because they *aren't*.

This has nothing to do with not loving him, but you have to be objective, even at times like this.

Tom was not a physically attractive proposition, what with the lumpy head, wrinkly skin and permanently baffled expression.

Also, new born babies aren't the most exciting things when you get right down to it.

It takes a few months before they doing anything other than scream, shit and puke - and you often sit there wishing they'd at least try to do something more productive.

Maybe I'm being a little unfair, but I never said I was a saint, did I?

We took Tom home after a day and settled into the business of raising a child in this hectic, cynical world.

Having a baby around really makes you appreciate the small things.

Sleep, for instance.

Never someone who has taken to sleep easily, I found the nightly routine of feeding and changing to be a never ending nightmare.

There I'd be, just slipping down the slippery chute to kipsville and Tom would start crying. That ear-piercing scream - so natural to him at his moment of birth - became more perfected in the next few months.

I started to think maybe he'd formed an unholy alliance with the birds outside; that the wood pigeon was periodically flying in through the window and giving him valuable advice about the best way to drive me insane. Teaching him lessons on the timing, rhythm, pitch and resonance of his scream that would combine to turn his father's brain into mulch as quickly as possible.

During the day, I'd start to enjoy the sound of silence more than ever.

Sitting in a quiet room, while Tom was asleep or his mother had taken him out, was a state of nirvana I appreciated at every opportunity.

Before my son, I would listen to pretty loud rock music as a way of relaxing. After he came along, the albums went into the cupboard and I grooved along to the sound of bugger all.

This hell lasted three months until Tom started sleeping through the night and my senses had become so deadened to the sounds of screaming I barely heard them anymore.

It's a good job I never passed a burning building in that time. My brain would have tuned out the pleading cries completely and I would have walked straight past without noticing.

As Tom grew, he became more interesting. He stopped being a lump - sitting there doing nothing much in particular.

I'm sure he won't go back to that kind of behaviour until he's a teenager.

Tom came out with his first word at about seven months.

To this day he's the kind of child that likes to be different. The first indication of this trait was the first word that came out of his mouth.

The usual words a baby says for the first time are along the lines of *mumma*, *dadda* or *nunna*. Easy words that require little effort - and make parents all misty eyed.

Not Tom though. No such simple pronouncements for him.

Tom's first word was 'Gorp'.

I swear to God... *Gorp*.

One minute nothing and the next *Gorp*.

Everything was Gorp.

I was Gorp. Sophie was Gorp. The house was Gorp. His nose was Gorp. Chickens were Gorp. Bruce Willis was Gorp. Contrails left by jumbo jets thirty thousand feet in the air were *Gorp*.

I began to worry.

I started to entertain the fantasy that Tom was not in fact my son, but was some kind of one man advance party for a massive alien invasion fleet.

Sophie had secretly been impregnated by these fiendish creatures and Tom's job was to let the whole world know the name of the monster who would become their alien master from beyond the stars.

Gorp.

Gorp The Mighty. Gorp The Powerful. Gorp The Emperor Of The Universe!

I kept an eye on Tom, waiting for him to start saying things like '*Gorp is coming. Bow down and kiss his tentacles*'.

This never happened, and Gorp's influence on my rapidly developing boy slowly slipped away. Gorp would have to invade our planet the old fashioned way, with big spaceships and lasers.

Tom then picked up the regular first few words with great speed. His pronunciation was never normal though. He never said *dadda*. It was always DAD - with a bold and clear tone of voice, which never failed to amuse me. The imperious way it would come out of his mouth made him sound like the Grand King Of Poobah-Land.

He'd also started to mimic sounds he'd hear.

It became a bit of an embarrassment when he picked up the word fuck. He no doubt caught this from me on one of the many occasions I tested his bath water and found it too hot, or tried to put a nappy on with cream all over my fingers.

Tom was like a parrot that sits in the corner of a room, shouting obscenities at anyone who comes into earshot.

There's nothing quite like the stony silence you get when your parents-in-law come round for a cup of tea and your kid starts swearing at them like a drunk Glaswegian docker.

There they are, sending you to sleep with their deadly dull recounting of their weekend in Eastbourne, when from the crib comes the epithet *fuck*, in a clear and ringing tone.

Repeatedly.

God knows what they thought I was doing to him. I'm sure they harboured visions of me crouched over his crib every evening, try to get him to repeat as many swear words as I could, possibly using cue cards and illustrations.

Tom walked at thirteen months.

Before that, he'd got around in a very deliberate and robotic crawling motion. With pudgy little hands clasped together, he'd put his elbows forward and pull himself along like a soldier crawling through the long grass, while a heavy fire fight goes on over head.

There's nothing guaranteed to put the willies up you more than waking from a nap to see your baby crawling inexorably towards you, repeating the word *Gorp* over and over in a low growl.

With walking came the barricading of the house to prevent injury.

My wife erected child proof gates at both ends of the stairs and in the kitchen doorway. They also went up in the doorways to the lounge, dining room and conservatory.

The house started to resemble a Stalag Luft designed for midgets.

I entertained images of lots of little fellas - like that bloke who works R2-D2 - secretly tunnelling under the house in a bid for freedom.

Tom would be leading them of course.

He'd have special instructions from Gorp on how to get out.

I thought these gates were overkill, but wasn't going to argue with Sophie. She became fiercely protective of Tom and would probably have murdered me in my sleep if I made the mistake of letting him bump his head while she wasn't around.

The gates proved no problem to Tom at all, who could open them easily after a few minutes careful contemplation - and would be delighted to see the look of abject horror on his mother's face when she caught him halfway up the stairs, teetering between one riser and the next.

Tom may have encountered no problem with the gates, but I bloody did.

One specific incident ended with me in hospital, a hairline fracture to the left wrist.

I'm not at my best first thing in the morning.

This is doubly true when I'm late for work.

In the first hour after waking my co-ordination isn't what it could be and nor is my memory.

I forgot all about the child proof gates at the top of the stairs.

I came rushing out of the bathroom at seven thirty in the morning, with toothpaste still around my mouth and my hair stuck up in wild clumps, thinking of the verbal kicking I was going to get for being late.

More immediate concerns, such as solid gates barring my path, were not in my head. The gate at the top of the stairs came as a complete surprise.

I hit the damn thing at full pelt and my body flipped over, like a gymnast performing a clumsy vault on the horse.

My arms went out in front as I shrieked at the top of my lungs.

Gravity did the ugly business of ensuring I hit the stairs as hard as possible.

My left leg got caught on the gate, slowing my speed and descent enough to change my injuries from *absolutely horrific* to just *pretty damn painful, actually*.

When I landed - cracking my wrist - and came to rest, I looked up the stairs with a dazed expression. Sophie, who had been with Tom, came out of his room and looked down at me.

I peered up at her shocked face for a second, before clumsily getting to my feet, supported on legs made of jelly. I told her in a quivering voice that I was alright, but it might be a good idea if I went to the hospital for a bit of a look over.

I was there for three hours – and had a good excuse for being late for work that day.

I got home that evening to find Sophie had taken down the gate at the top of the stairs and put it across the door to Tom's room. When I went to give him a kiss goodnight, he favoured me with an expression that seemed to say 'Yeah, thanks a lot for that. Now I really am a prisoner. You just wait until I see Gorp.'

It saddens me to say that my experience of Tom's mental and physical development was cut short when Sophie and I divorced.

While I'm still able to see him, I don't have the continuity that comes with being in the same house all the time.

I try to look on the bright side and think that for the most part I'm getting the pleasurable highlights, while Sophie has to deal with the tantrums and naughtiness.

But who am I kidding? I'd give anything to be around for those too.

I see enough of my son to make the pain of missing him bearable and I love doing things like taking him to the park - to watch him run around the field chasing invisible friends.

I always appreciate these times and pay special attention, because they're not as common as I'd like.

That's partly why I'm able to write this, because whenever I'm with Tom, I soak up the experience and memorise the details. They're very clear in my mind, so it's no trouble to put them down on a page.

Kids grow up fast and if you don't commit all the funny incidents and sweet moments to memory, you'll find yourself unable to remember how gorgeous and wonderful they were as children - rather than as they are now: seventeen, miserable and hating your guts.

It helps to have a camera on stand by a lot.

Not only will you take lots of pictures of them in their charming infancy to look at in later years, it also gives you something to embarrass them with when they bring their first dates home to meet you when they're fourteen and only mildly *dislike* your guts.

Whenever I think of my relationship with Tom, I always end up asking myself the same question:

Am I a good father?

It's the question of a man naturally disposed to neuroticism.

I think I am. I certainly *hope* I am.

Despite the fact I'm not around twenty four-seven, I'd like to think I provide the kind of support a father should give their child.

I never wonder if Sophie is a good mother or not, I know she is.

That makes my dilemma worse...

It'd be far easier to claim that I was a good dad if I didn't have to compare myself to the high standards Sophie sets.

I spent a huge amount of time until a year or so ago dwelling on this and never reached a satisfactory answer. I'd weigh up the pros and cons ad infinitum, until I ended up confusing myself no end.

The answer I finally arrived at is simplicity itself:

Whether I'm there enough of the time, whether I handle discipline properly, whether I provide a good example or not, I know I love my kid to bits.

As far as I'm concerned, that *does* make me a good father.

Perfect?

Absolutely not.

But I'll always care, and I'll always be there for him.

For me, that defines what love for a child should be.

Even when the little bastard is drawing on the sofa.

Fanfare please!

We've reached the twenty four hour mark! Well, we did twenty five minutes ago, but I was too busy writing about Tom to notice.

Who'd have thought it, eh?

That I'd be able to sustain this project for an entire twenty four hours without rest?

Excellent!

I had my doubts. I bet you did to.

It was touch and go there for a while - back in the cold, dark watches of the night. And you'll notice from the time checks that I've slowed down in terms of productivity per hour.

But I'm still going. Just like that bunny in the battery advert from a few years ago.

Part of that is down to you, my friend.

Without having you sat there, prompting me to greater heights of creativity, I imagine I'd have quit after three hours and gone to watch some porn or the Saturday night movie.

I'd have probably sat through Armageddon in a grumpy mood, knowing that I hadn't stayed the distance, and would have gone to bed in a huff, cursing my lack of will-power.

But instead, here I am - all down to you, my muse and confidant.

Thank you.

Let's examine my general state of well being, then:

Hmmm. Peckish.

Not just peckish actually, but *starving*.

I shall now nip quickly to the kitchen to rustle up some grub.

Anything you fancy? Or should I just grab as much as I can from the cupboard?

…yeah, I thought you'd prefer that.

I know you've got a thing for cookies, so I'll take a look and see if there are any.

…

Nope, no cookies. Sorry.

But, we do now have half a barbecue chicken to pick clean and some of that strange ham with slices of egg in the middle.

How do they do that? It's like putting the egg in scotch eggs - a complete mystery.

There's some bread and a nice jar of sandwich pickle. The one with small chunks, so the sandwich doesn't look like the surface of the moon when you've finished making it.

There's a bottle of Diet Coke there as well - with cherry in. I though it would taste disgusting - like the lemon one does - but the geniuses at the Coca-Cola Company have come up trumps on this one. Very tasty indeed.

With our refreshments in front of us, let's examine the thorny topic of self-analysis.

It's a pretty good subject to tackle, as we're all guilty of doing it at one time or another.

I've already answered the question of whether I'm a good father to the best of my ability - it's up to you to decide if I did it well or not - but there are plenty more questions of its type rolling around my head, creating a dreadful racket.

Here's a few examples:

Am I nice?
Am I attractive?
Am I a good writer?
Am I respected by my peers?
Am I good in bed?
Am I thinking too much?

Answers on a back of a postcard, please.

As you can never really arrive at conclusive answers to these questions - with maybe the exception of the last one - it's a more valid use of your time to wonder why you ask them in the first place.

It's back to that human nature thing, isn't it?

We're all cursed with questioning our lot in life and how we could make it better: How we could be better looking, better dressed and more sophisticated at cocktail parties - instead of nibbling on a few dry canapés, getting blitzed and spending the entire evening talking to a pot plant.

Darwinian followers will stroke their beards and say its part of survival of the fittest, which drives the engine of human achievement - and they may well be right.

If we're analysing our faults and trying to do something about fixing them, then we're trying to lift ourselves above those around us. Trying to reach the top of the tree where all the best bananas are, so to speak.

I'd argue there's more to it than that, though.

Part of the reason we obsess about ourselves is because the world we live in *makes* us.

Take a good look around next time you step out of the front door. Make a mental list of the amount of times you see something that preys on your self-esteem.

Bet you get to at least fifty in a day.

Here's the most prevalent example:

Am I attractive?

Well… *are you*?

Looking at advertising hoardings and magazines it would appear you're *not*, actually - and neither am I.

If we were, there wouldn't be so many companies trying to sell us products that are meant improve our looks.

There wouldn't be as many posters featuring beautiful, air-brushed models, mugging away to the camera - convincing us that we just *have* to buy this new shampoo that makes your hair look like silk and feel stronger than steel.

Having it smell like peach, persimmon or apple blossom appears to be a must too - though why anyone would want to walk around with a head smelling like a fruit basket is beyond me.

We're constantly bombarded with this kind of thing.

Some of us try to ignore these messages and some embrace them whole-heartedly.

Eventually though, pretty much everyone succumbs to the pressure of our peers and the advertising companies. We buy the products and read the lifestyle tips in the magazines, hoping they'll make us better people.

I've done it.

I've bought the deodorant that's supposed to make me a sex magnet. I've worn the clothes designed to make me look rich and successful. I've eaten the food meant to make me look fit and full of vitality.

Yet for some reason, as I sit here, I'm not surrounded by super-models.

Nor am I filthy rich.

Could it just *possibly* be that these messages are – gasp! - *wrong*? That all the adverts and all the lifestyle gurus are comprehensively and utterly *full of shit*?

There are no supermodels and no vast sums of money nearby, but I *do* have a slight paunch that will turn into an unsightly gut if I'm not careful.

Strange…

Could this be down to the fact that while half the consumer industry is telling us to buy products meant to make us look better and feel healthier - the other half are selling us stuff that makes us fat, unhealthy and unattractive again?

Chocolate, fast food, cigarettes, booze, sweets - the list goes on and on.

I smell a conspiracy!

Is it any wonder most of us are confused, when we're being bombarded with such conflicting ideologies?

Buy this pizza and we'll make you fat!
Buy this ab-cruncher and we'll make you thin!

Hell, why not eat your pizza while using the ab-cruncher at the same time!

You'll achieve a Zen-like harmony between two states of being and will probably transcend to a higher level of existence. At that point they can sell religion to you as well!

Good grief.

How many times have you had the following experience?

You're doing your weekly shop and find yourself poised over the freezer cabinet trying to decide between the *Good For You* range of meals that you don't really want, but will stop you turning into Jabba The Hutt - and the full fat *Incredibly Bad For You* range that tastes nice, but will pile on the calories.

What an enormous ball ache.

I tend to buy both in an agony of indecision, which is fast becoming a real strain on my wallet.

I've even stood looking at food packets for the calorie content. I nearly started taking a calculator to the store with me, but as that would make me the world's saddest twat, I left it at home - inside the diary I got for Christmas.

Inevitably, I end up eating all the full fat stuff and the healthy food rots gently in the back of the cupboard, or enters its own private ice age in the freezer.

I joined a gym last year - try not to look at my curved back and aforementioned gut, please. If you do, try to stifle the laughter, my ego can't take it. I joined in January, in an attempt to keep a new year's resolution for once in my life and lose a few pounds.

The place was recommended to me by a sickeningly healthy friend, who assured me that their rates were cheap and they'd give me *buns of steel* in no time at all.

Along I go, with my credit card held high, hoping for a better - and more muscular - future.

The gym was a lovely place.

Full of spangly, complicated looking work-out equipment, tanned and healthy staff, cheerful lighting and the positive atmosphere of a place built solely for the purpose of making bodies slimmer and bank accounts empty.

There were motivational posters all over the walls, featuring superhuman young men and women in a variety of action poses on exercise equipment.

Slogans were writ large across them, such as:

'One day at a time = A better life!'
'Change your style, Change your attitude, Change your future!'

Frankly, it was the kind of propaganda that would have made Joseph Goebbels cry with delight.

Happily, there wasn't one up that said *There's No 'I' In Team!* - otherwise my visit to the gym would have been very short-lived.

Violent, but short-lived.

Essentially, this gym was the kind of place that encouraged you to put in the effort and come back time and again to enjoy the thrill of healthy exercise.

…I went three times.

The first was a half an hour orientation evening, when I was completely baffled by everything the pretty, lycra-clad girl told me. I may have no problem using some electronic gadgets, but when it comes to exercise bicycles and rowing machines, I'm a Luddite of the highest order.

She was quite patient with me, explaining what all the buttons and blinking lights did. I nodded my head and took in none of it.

It didn't help that she had a magnificent pair of breasts.

If I'd had a calendar with those on, the car would never have got through its M.O.T.

I went home that night with a feeling of trepidation about using any of the infernal machines, but was determined to see it through and achieve buns of steel as quickly as possible.

Second time round I was on my own.

The pretty girl who'd given me the grand tour was in the gym that night, but was far too caught up in a conversation with a tree-trunk of a man who looked like he was permanently in the middle of a body building competition. His breasts were slightly bigger than hers.

Having changed, I ventured into the exercise room in my brand new jogging pants and muscle vest. I only looked *marginally* ridiculous, and fitted in well with the rest of the spandex squad.

The look was only ruined by the tatty trainers I had on my feet.

I was willing to spend twenty quid in Marks and Sparks on my new found fitness hobby, but I didn't fancy forking out eighty quid for a new pair of Reeboks.

...this says a lot about my level of commitment.

I'd also toyed with the idea of wearing a headband, but thought better of it.

I started my workout gently with the treadmill.

I can work a treadmill, no problem. The amount of buttons on the keypad may be high, but you can't go far wrong with a machine that's basically a glorified hamster wheel and only has three settings: slow, fast and heart attack inducing.

Setting it on slow, I began to jog my way to a life without love handles.

I was under the illusion that many unfit people have when they come to a place like this.

Because I was in a *proper* gym, using *proper* gym equipment, the state of my unfitness would therefore be miraculously off-set by the professional atmosphere and technological wizardry at my disposal. I may smoke nearly twenty a day and think getting out of bed in the morning constitutes a sit-up, but all these lovely gadgets would compensate completely.

And besides, I look like a fit person in my muscle shirt and joggers, so I should *feel* like one too!

Here I was, paying out a couple of hundred quid for a year's use of the facilities, so surely my body would respond to my over-whelming generosity toward it and raise its game a bit.

Needless to say, this didn't happen.

After five minutes on the treadmill, I'm wheezing - and after fifteen I sound like a dying camel.

This really wasn't going well at all.

People start to look round to see where all the noise is coming from, possibly expecting the gym to have suddenly filled with silent Bedouins, accompanying the camel that's stumbled in from the Gobi desert.

The sweat starts to run down my face in rivulets.

My leg muscles are aching like mad.

I should have stopped, I really should have. But by this time, I'm aware I've something of an audience watching - and pride takes over.

Instead of getting off the treadmill and taking a much needed rest, I actually *turn up the speed.*

'Hey everyone! I may look like I'm running closer and closer to death with every second that passes, but in actual fact, I'm just getting started! The laboured breathing is just a cunning ploy to make you think I don't know what I'm doing! But I must, because I've just turned up the speed!'

With the treadmill now on fast, my legs are pumping harder than they have in fifteen years.

The look of agony on my face is palpable. It's the grinning rictus of a man possessed by his own stupidity.

I'm now wheezing like a camel in a gas-mask.

My body starts to rebel and I begin to lose co-ordination in my arms and legs.

I'm not so much running now as I am permanently *falling forward*.

Out of the corner of my eye, I can see the pretty gym girl calling the paramedics, showing a real talent for forward planning.

Everyone else is starting to edge away from my wildly flailing body, so they're outside the flight path when inertia finally catches up and sling-shots me off the treadmill into the nearest wall.

I want to stop now, I really do. But my vision is blurred so much and my arms are so totally out of control that I'm unable to use the treadmill's keypad to stop the thing.

It wouldn't have mattered anyway, as by now I haven't got a clue how to work it. My brain ceased to function with any clarity about two minutes ago.

There's an inevitable end to a situation like this and it's never a happy one.

So far, I've managed to keep my legs pointing in the right direction. This changes just as I think my heart is going to jump out of my mouth and slope off for a nice quiet cup of coffee, leaving the rest of me to it.

My legs buckle and I wobble about on the treadmill like a three hundred mile an hour drunk.

The top half of my body is thrown *forward*, while the bottom half is catapulted *backward* by the maniacal treadmill.

It also flings me off to the side, which I'm grateful for as it saves me head-butting the bar in front.

In a freakish defiance of all the laws of physics, I hurtle sideways, forwards, backwards and upwards *all at once* - clearing the treadmill with exactly the opposite amount of grace a fourteen year old Russian gymnast has when dismounting the parallel bars.

Amazingly, I land on my feet. Quite how, I don't know. I guess the laws of physics have by now given up on the whole debacle and gone to join my heart at Starbucks for a latté and a doughnut.

I don't stay on my feet for long and collapse onto the nearby weights bench.

I look up and can see some people are still watching me with a mixture of amusement and concern.

Bastards.

It's like none of them ever had a first session at the gym and nearly killed themselves trying to over-achieve. I won't give them the satisfaction of watching me buckle!

I should have got my breath back and limped off into the changing rooms, giving up the fight there and then - but I didn't.

My body was distraught, but my brain was full of angry determination.

The brain won by a technical knock-out.

Instead of doing the sensible thing and leaving, I start lifting weights.

What a fucking *idiot*.

As my eyesight still wasn't firing on all cylinders, it took me a few moments to set the right amount of weight I thought I could manage in a bench press.

I stretched myself out on the bench, clasped the bar and tried to lift.

And tried a bit more...

And a bit more...

By now my face is the same colour as a baboon's arse and my eyes are standing two inches out from their sockets.

I reset the weight to a more acceptable amount - half what it was - and try again.

This time, the bar goes up and I start to feel like Arnold Schwarzenegger as I pump away merrily. The fact a nine year old girl could have probably lifted the amount I had on there didn't trouble me in the least.

I got to about twenty reps (see? I know all the technical terms) before something went *twang!* in my back.

The pain was *horrendous*.

I didn't cry out, but I'm fairly sure the low, plaintive whine that came out of my mouth carried across the gym anyway.

The weights came back down with a crash as I finally – *finally* – gave up the struggle and accepted my fate.

I stayed on the bench for a good couple of minutes, doing half-arsed stretches with my arms to hide the fact that I could barely move the rest of my body.

Eventually, when I'd decided most of my audience had gone back to toning their buns of steel, I got up and made my crippled way back to the locker room.

Have you seen Dawn Of The Dead?

I would have made a fantastic addition to the film's cast.

I groaned and limped my way to the sanctuary of the changing room, not turning my head to look at my fellow exercisers. This wasn't because I was trying to ignore them, it was because turning my head was virtually impossible.

It took me over twenty minutes to get changed into my street clothes - each movement punctuated with a low mewling noise and a series of shooting pains down my back.

Leaving the building and getting into my car, I vowed that next time - if there was a next time - I'd take things a bit easier and ignore the sneers and superior looks of the annoyingly hyper-fit gym denizens.

It took me two weeks to recover from my second trip to the gym, before returning for the third and final time.

Nothing horrendous occurred. I'd learned my lessons and didn't intend to repeat the same mistakes again.

Clad in the same keep fit get-up as before, I re-entered the scene of my brush with death, intent on getting something worthwhile out of the experience.

Luckily, the gym was nearly empty.

Well, it wasn't luck, really. I just went at half past nine in the evening on a Tuesday, when I knew the place would be deserted.

Things went well for a while.

I used the treadmill again and managed a good ten minutes of light jogging before the black dots appeared in front of my eyes. I did a spot of rowing, which made me feel very manly and a bit like Sir Steve Redgrave.

I ran into trouble - of the psychological kind, rather the physical - when I came to use the nautilus machine.

This, for those of you that don't know, is a contraption of pure evil.

It's a multi-use piece of high resistance weight lifting equipment that looks like a medieval torture device. The type of thing that'd give Torquemada a hard-on.

Undeterred, I sallied forth into my nautilus experience with cheer in my heart and passion in my soul.

I got into the thing easily and it only took a second to figure out how to use it: Insert arms here, place legs here, thrust and repeat.

I elected for the full nautilus work out and started to do leg presses, as well as butterfly crunches with my arms.

I was sweating. I was pumping. I was achieving the buns of steel I'd been promised.

There was a bank of large mirrors on the wall opposite me.

The kind I'm sure are just ever so slightly warped to make you think you're wider than you really are.

Everything was hunky dory until I caught sight of myself in that mirror.

There I was, arms and legs akimbo like a puppy dog on its back, waiting for a tickle. My hair was stood up in sweaty spikes and the baggy muscle shirt I wore did nothing to accent my physique in the slightest. I was also red-faced and grimacing.

My exercise hobby came to an end at that moment.

Yes, I may have been working the *glutes* and toning the *abs*.

Yes, I may have been burning calories and losing fat.

But none of that mattered.

I looked at myself in the mirror and saw with horror that while I was in fitness heaven, I also looked like *a complete prick*.

I glanced at the small group of people also using the gym and they looked like pricks too. A collection of sweating, heaving hamsters, caught in the machinery of ridiculous exercise bikes, rowers and stair-masters.

Here we all were, otherwise sane and rational people, spending our valuable free time in monotonous and repetitive activity, trying to achieve a physical image created by advertising executives in order to sell us after-shave and perfume.

'*Oh my God! What the hell am I doing!?*'

An epiphany like this cannot be ignored.

I got off the accursed nautilus machine, stormed out of the gym and changed into my street clothes, mumbling various comments about the stupidity of the world under my breath.

I left the gym for the final time and went home.

When I got there I stuck a movie on and ordered a kebab.

It was the best tasting pound of cholesterol I've ever had.

The practical upshot is:

While there's benefit in taking gentle exercise and watching what you eat, spending a fortune and all your time behaving like a small, furry rodent for the sake of losing a couple of pounds is as pointless as trying to drink the Pacific with a straw.

And anyone who says different?

Fuck 'em.

Life's too short and so is my patience.

I went off on a bit of a rant there.

Apologies.

I hope your feelings are similar, though.

I think the world probably needs more people who don't obey the rules, just because it's the done thing.

These rules were made up by very greedy people in multi-national companies, intent on separating us from our hard earned pennies.

If you're fat, thin, short, tall, greasy, hairy, pale or any number of things they tell us we shouldn't be, but *you're happy with who you are*, then don't get caught in their web!

Live free, live large and I'll see you down the kebab shop!

Not that you'll be very hungry right now, seeing as that poor barbecued chicken has been stripped to the bone.

I didn't get that much, you know...

With all the cookies you've been eating as well, you might start showing a little bit of extra padding around the middle if you're not careful. Having said that, I can see you've taken my advice to heart and aren't going to worry about such things.

Good for you!

There's a few digestives left if you're up for them.

I've really warmed to you as my muse over the past twenty six hours.

You seem to be an intelligent, up-standing member of society that I'd be glad to vote for in any elections you might want to run in.

I'm almost jealous.

Good grief.

I'm comparing myself to someone I can't see, can't hear and is at least several months into the future from now.

I think the lack of sleep has made me a little nuts.

You have to stop me from doing stuff like that, you know. Endlessly comparing myself to others - real or imaginary - and worrying whether I match up or not.

If I carry on, I'll lose all confidence and this book will dribble to an inconclusive halt.

Self confidence is a hard thing to come by when you're as prone to neurotic thoughts as me, so deciding whether I'm better than the next person is a big mistake.

Especially if the next guy is Steve McQueen. Yes, I know he's dead, but I'm pretty sure he's *still* cooler than I am.

I have a friend I met during my amateur dramatic days - short-lived as they were - who had confidence you could bounce large and pointy rocks off.

He's an actor and I suppose its necessary for that kind of profession - but it gets a bit grating after a while.

Nothing troubles him.

His name's Max and when Max is in a room, he's automatically the centre of attention, steam-rolling his way through conversations with a sublime indifference to what those around him are thinking.

I don't know whether it's a good personality trait or not.

You may end up offending people, but if you don't care, you won't spend hours agonising about it afterwards, so who gives a monkeys?

I admire Max and loathe him in equal measure - but he's good for a laugh and when I'm with him I never have to worry that people are analysing me for faults, because I'm very much the background extra, while he's the featured lead.

I'm fairly sure my penis is larger than his though, which gives me some solace.

Max is trying to get a career off the ground and I wish him every success.

He's certainly got the attitude for the job – where a degree of self-assurance about your abilities is vital if you're going to get over the rejections that come with endless auditioning.

Everyone wants to be a success, of course.

I've never met anyone that's said to me:

'No, no, I don't want to be successful and popular. I'd be much happier to face failure at every turn, because I believe it makes me a better person.'

If you do know anyone like that, do them a favour and put them out of their misery.

Success is what we all strive for: with our jobs, with the opposite sex, with our hobbies, with our talent, with money.

Money.

That's a biggie, isn't it?

Our culture supports the idea that having a big pile of cash means you're a success, and can safely ignore the little people on your drive to the country club in the Aston Martin.

We're supposed to look up to the rich and down on the poor, aren't we?

The more glitzy and expensive stuff someone has, the more the world sees them as being the bee's knees, the dog's danglies, *the mutt's nuts*.

In short: a better person.

Is there a better way of demonstrating how wonderful you are than having a sports car in the drive, a yacht in the harbour and a set of gleaming white teeth moths like to circle round at night?

It's what we all aspire to because at some point it was decided that material wealth was the way people should be judged.

...I must have missed that meeting.

If you can't earn the money, you can always play the lottery.

Yeah.

There's a real winner of an idea.

The National Lottery had the strap-line:

It Could Be You!

This should probably have been revised to reflect the reality of the situation:

It Could Be You! ...but it probably won't be, you nasty little person!

No, it probably won't. Odds of fourteen million to one against guarantee it.

The only silver lining is the fact that you know full well that while you haven't won, nobody you know has won either.

You'd have no problem with a friend or loved one cashing in, but somebody who really pisses you off?

That'd be *awful.*

There you are, buying your tickets every Wednesday and Saturday, winning jack-shit and Carol from Accounts - who you've hated since she grassed on you for claiming too much overtime last year - wins quarter of a million and fucks off to Barbados for a month.

Wouldn't that just make you spit?

Especially if Carol was one of those idiots who say things like this when they win the lottery:

'Oh no, I won't quit my job! I love what I do!'

What are you, *mental*?

They'll make the argument that there's no point in them quitting work, as they enjoy it and its stress free.

Well, of course it's stress free, you've just won the flaming lottery!!

You don't care about your job anymore because the monthly wage you earn is now less than the interest that big, fat mountain of cash you've just lucked into is accruing in your Swiss bank account!

Not only does someone you hate win the lottery, they also have the gall to come back to work and rub your nose in it.

In they stride, wearing a two thousand pound leather jacket, a four hundred pound haircut and twirling the keys to the Ferrari parked out front.

They may buy everyone in the office a nice meal at the local Harvester, but it would have been much nicer if they'd just buggered off to Barbados permanently and left the rest to carry on working, watching the clock on the wall and groaning at 6.30 every Monday morning.

You can bet your bottom dollar that the people who'd carry on working after winning the lottery are *also* the ones who come into work when they're sick, the ones who set the time on their alarm clocks five minutes earlier and the type to say you could never quit smoking.

It's a club, you know.

They have meetings where they think of new ways to annoy the rest of us. When I find the club house, I'm going to burn the fucker to the ground.

Don't get me wrong, I don't hate rich people.

Jealous of them? *yes*. Hate them? *no*.

I just don't like rich folk who make a big deal out of being minted.

It's not classy.

The only analogy I can draw from personal experience is if I went around showing people my sizeable chopper at every opportunity.

That wouldn't be classy at all.

Illegal, as well.

…fun at weddings, though.

Here's a tip:

Don't bother being envious of people who have more money than you. You don't know how they got it and don't know whether the rest of their life is crap or not. Just comparing their bank balance with yours isn't a true indicator of how you stack up against them as a human being.

The same goes for how other people look as well:

She's got bigger boobs than you? So what? She's probably got the IQ of an ice cube.

He's got bigger muscles than you? To Hell with it! He probably has body odour that'd knock out an elephant.

The next time you find yourself comparing body parts or bank balances, just imagine some really nasty defect for them. That'll equal things out a bit.

On one of my overseas trips I visited the one place on the planet where your worth as a human being is *definitely* dictated by how much money you put on display. Where plastic is fantastic and never mind about those troublesome brain cells.

Hollywood.

More specifically we're talking Beverly Hills, a place where the faces are stretched, the breasts are fake and the eyes are vacant.

I was enjoying a stroll down Rodeo Drive, looking in the shop windows and trying to contain my amazement that anyone would charge several thousand dollars for a small rug with a zigzag pattern on it.

These were the days when smoking a cigarette in L.A wouldn't immediately get you locked up in the nearest penitentiary with Bubba, the three hundred pound sex pervert. I sparked up as I strolled along, polluting this most rarefied of atmospheres.

From behind me I hear a very nasal *'Excuse me?'*

I turn to find myself confronted with a human lizard in a bright yellow Chanel outfit, with matching handbag and shoes.

Shielding my eyes from the onslaught of colour, I approached with curiosity.

'Yes? Can I help?' I said, in a faintly amused voice.

The woman - I think it was a woman. It may have been a gecko, I couldn't quite tell - heard my accent and her face lit up in a frightful way that pulled her already over-stretched skin even further back on her skull.

'Oh! You're English!' she exclaimed, in a high-pitched Californian twang.

Oh dear.

If you've British and have never been to America, but intend to go some time in the future, expect this kind of conversation at least once.

'Yes, I am.'

'Oh, I luuurve the English!'

'That's nice.'

'They're my favourite foreign people, because they speak English and like Americans.'

Well, you're certainly right on the first point there, love. Not too sure about the second one these days. Mind you, at least you got rid of that maniac Bush and replaced him with some who actually has a brain.

The lizard switches track at this point, remembering why she's accosted me in the first place, and produces what looks like a solid gold cigarette holder from a solid gold Chanel handbag and puts a solid gold cigarette into it.

This all screams:

I have money! Lots of lovely money!

'Can I have a light?' she asked, squinting at me in the mid-morning sun.

I flip open the Zippo and provide her with fire.

She gratefully sucks at it through the cigarette holder and lets out a plume of smoke smelling vaguely of coffee. That's how you know a cigarette's expensive - when it stinks of something it probably shouldn't.

'I love England,' she continues, not intent on letting me go until she's had her say. 'My husband and I like to go shopping in London.'

Like to go *shopping* in London.

Not on *holiday* to London... oh no.

She treats travelling half-way across the world in first class in the same way we'd treat popping down town on a Saturday afternoon to pick up some new shelves from B&Q.

I'm at a loss for a response – which happens rarely. How do you provide a comeback to a statement like that?

'That's nice for you,' I eventually mumble. 'I went to London to see Cats a few months ago.'

A brilliant piece of small talk, I'm sure you'll agree.

Frankly, I want to get away from Godzilla as soon as possible. The smell of her cigarette is starting to make me nauseous and I'm going slightly blind from the sun reflecting off the yellow outfit.

I say a perfunctory goodbye and make my exit - feigning interest in the nice rug with zigzags on it I've seen in a nearby shop window.

Meeting this aging monster made me feel a lot better about myself.

It's true I can't afford to hop on a plane to New York and do a spot of browsing round JC Penney, but it's also true that my eyes don't constantly water due to face-lifts and I don't look like a lizard in a hideous outfit that advertises some pompous fashion label.

I've met people like this many times. Not quite to her extent maybe, but displaying many of the same traits.

I work in marketing after all and it's a business that sees the little man – me - come up against the big man - fat, sweaty pharmaceutical giant - on many occasions.

Comparisons with the well-to-do are unavoidable sometimes, especially when you're working your way up the employment ladder to the dizzy heights of a private parking space and twenty weeks holiday a year.

Now I'm older, wiser and a heap-load more cynical, I like to ignore the material aspect of my fellow man and judge them purely on their actions.

Then if I happen to see some guy in a flash car and an even flasher suit, I'll wait to see what kind of man he is up close and personal before I decide whether I like him and want to *be* like him or not.

Ten times out of ten so far, I've discovered *I don't*.

I've never met anyone with a great personality that also liked to show off their wealth and success - but the search goes on.

What's that? Did I hear you mumble 'pigs might fly'?

You know what?

I'm running out of stuff to talk about.

If I carry on much longer I'm going to start repeating myself and that'll do us no good at all.

Covered a lot though, haven't we?

Love, marriage, children, work and malfunctioning bowels to name a few.

We've been back and forth through time, dipping into Spalding's life at random moments to glimpse past incidents that have served to highlight a point, explain how I think and bring on a chuckle or two.

Now we're in the final downhill run, careering towards a conclusion at break-neck speed with no concern for our own safety.

At the beginning I said starting was easy and keeping going was the hard bit. I'm now starting to think that ending might be tricky, too.

Not much new there, eh?

How many times do we find it hard to end something? How many times do we feel sad when something comes to a conclusion?

If you're the one to end a relationship it's never easy, because you feel the guilt of upsetting the other party. Or, if they've turned out to be a nutcase it can be difficult, because you don't want them to put your favourite pet in a bubbling pot of water, or write nasty things about you on toilet doors.

Switch it around and you're the one being dumped. Is there anything more horrible than a relationship ending that you've been happy with?

How about leaving a job?

That can be hard, if its one you enjoy.

Even if the new job pays better and is nearer to your house.

If you've built up friendships at the place you've worked for the last seven years, then it's bound to be difficult to wander off into the sunset without a pang of regret.

Even short term things can be hard to finish:

The fantastic week's holiday you've just had in Morocco for instance, where you wandered through the bazaars, chatted up the local skirt and drank too much alcohol.

I always have problems when I come back from a trip abroad and have to slide back into normal life.

It also takes me ages to get the pictures downloaded onto the laptop, as if that last exercise is the final indication the holiday is actually over.

What about the end of the Christmas break, if you're lucky enough to get one?

There are no happy people in this world at the beginning of January. With the exception of gym owners, perhaps.

Getting more short term:

What about the great parties on a Saturday night, where the music rocks, the booze is free and you're surrounded by like-minded people who won't take the piss too much if you crap yourself in public. Problem is, you know the party has to end sometime and that Monday morning is looming on the horizon …

That's the reason why so many Saturday night parties go on until five or six in the morning. It may seem like it's because everyone is so tanked up that the clock has become just a blurry blob on the periphery of vision, but it's actually because we know damn well that the clock is there and we're trying our best to deny its existence by staying up well past our bedtime.

Let's get *really* short-term shall we?

Watching a good movie.

Sat in a comfy seat at the multiplex, popcorn in one hand and bucket of coke in the other, you sit and watch some amazing spectacle unfold in front of you. You love the characters, you love the plot. It speaks to you in ways no other film ever has.

But you know it has to end – and that very soon you'll be spending fifteen minutes trying to find the BMW in a car park roughly the size of Mozambique.

Even more short term?

How about lunch breaks in the sun, with a tasty baguette from the sandwich shop and a cup of coffee that revives and invigorates? You eat the baguette and sip the coffee, knowing full well you've got to go back to that bloody processing report in a minute.

What about a long, luxurious bath?

The tub is full with hot soapy water that soothes away aches and pains. No-one else is in the house, so you're able to giggle loudly when you fart and can sing songs at the top of your voice if you want. But the water will get cold eventually and you'll have to get out.

How about the half an hour you spend reading a good book?

The one by Nick Spalding that you downloaded because it looked like an easy read. You've found it to be a thoroughly entertaining way to pass a few minutes in your otherwise hectic schedule and would recommend it to your friends.

...*ahem*.

Shorter term *still*:

How about the first cigarette after a large and delicious meal?

Or the last drink before saying goodbye to your friends and wending your way home in the spring moonlight?

Or the soaring orgasm you have at the same time as the person you love?

When all good things end, it's hard (or soft in the last example) and there's inevitably some sadness and pain involved.

In a way, that's good though, isn't it?

After all, there's nothing wrong with the flavour bitter-sweet...

Nearly at the end now…

Only a few pages left.

Stick with me. I still have a few things to get off my chest before we're done.

So, what should you do with this book when you've finished it?

You could simply stick it on your bookshelf, leaving it to electronically hibernate.

If you do, please do me a favour and don't store it next to some weighty, important novel like Of Mice And Men or The Complete Works Of Shakespeare. It'll be highly embarrassing to be in such company and I may never recover.

The next time someone asks you if you've got anything to read, you can suggest this book if you like. Don't give them your copy though, make them download one of their own and I'll share the royalties with you 50/50. Deal?

Alternatively:

Top Tips For What To Do With Spalding's Book Once You've Finished It!

1. Flog it at a car boot sale. Make sure you break the spine and rough it up a bit. People are more likely to buy a second hand book if it looks used – assuming that if a lot of other people have read it, then it must be a pretty spiffy read. For a bit of fun, start the price off at a ridiculously high level and see if you get any takers. Then drop it down to ten pence two hours later when you inevitably don't.

2. Someone in this world you don't like? Then why not highlight the passages in bold that you feel best describe them. I've taken a pop at all different kinds of people over the last fifty thousand words, so there's hopefully a suitable section you can use. When you do this, point meaningfully at the parts you've highlighted and say *'read and learn.'*

163

3. Get me to autograph your copy. This will require stalking me for an extended period of time. I tend to go for a constitutional walk around tea time if that helps. When you've finally confronted me and I steadfastly refuse to sign, threaten me with a sponge until I capitulate.

4. Deliberately annoy people at dinner parties by entering into a conversation about a topic I've brought up. When they start to make a point, whip out your copy and utter *'Well, Nick Spalding says...'* followed by a lengthy reading in a dull, monotonous voice. See how many times you can do this in one evening before they throw you out.

5. Decide this book is now your Bible. Take it down the local shopping mall and stand reciting parts of it at the top of your voice until the police come along and batter you with truncheons. Call them fascist thugs between beatings. If nothing else, you'll probably get on YouTube.

6. Spend months looking for the secret code in the text that will lead you to a complete understanding of the nature of existence. If it works for Dan Brown, it can work for me. If you do find anything, bore intellectual people with it at your leisure.

7. Translate the book into a foreign language. Compare the two versions and learn a new tongue. You'll know the Swahili for clock, sponge, bowels and embarrassment in no time, I assure you.

8. Need to make an apology to a loved one for a recent indiscretion? Rip out the following section, filling in the blanks as appropriate:

I, _____ AM VERY SORRY
FOR_____LAST WEEK/MONTH/YEAR
(delete as appropriate).

I WHOLE-HEARTEDLY APOLOGISE, AND HOPE THAT YOU'RE ABLE TO FORGIVE ME/ LET ME OFF/ NOT CUT ME OUT OF YOUR WILL/ GET THE PROBLEM CLEARED UP WITH OINTMENTS (delete as appropriate) AS SOON AS POSSIBLE.

THE AUTHOR NICK SPALDING WILL BACK ME UP ON MY SINCERITY, AND YOU CAN TRUST HIS OPINION COMPLETELY.

SIGNED, IN GROVELLING REGRET:_____

9. Use this book as inspiration to write your own. I'm certainly too lazy to write a sequel, so why not take up the mantle for me? As I've said, people love to read about the lives of others and I'm sure you have quite a few anecdotes of your own that'll fill up a couple of hundred pages. I recommend doing it in intervals over a few weeks though. This writing a whole book in one sitting thing sounds like a nice idea, but you try telling that to my arse.

There you go, not only do you get a book to read, you also get some helpful tips and suggestions for hobbies and pastimes - I like to add that extra special something when I can.

So we've come to the end of our journey.

You've been here by my side through the entire thing and I genuinely hope it's been fun for you.

I hope you've liked the time we've spent together - and that the chair you've been sitting in for what seems like a century hasn't destroyed your posterior completely.

You've enjoyed the food, of that there is no doubt, and you've been very good at not complaining about the smoke from the endless stream of cigarettes. Their ranks have dwindled and many soldiers have fallen in battle, with my lungs now a blasted wasteland.

The coffee was crap, but then what drink wouldn't be when it's been standing in a thermos flask for hours?

I hope I've made you chuckle.

I truly believe that if you can laugh at past mistakes or current difficulties, it can make the shadows they cast in your life *just a bit smaller.*

Most of all, I hope the time you've spent with me has been a pleasant way to ignore the clock on the wall, with its infernal ticks and tocks.

If I've managed to do that, I'm one happy writer.

I hope you had a good time, my friend.

As far as I'm concerned, I've had the time of my life.

I'm now going to sleep for about three hundred years - or until the birds wake me up, which ever comes first.

All the best,
Nick.

The End
55124 Words

About the author:

Nick Spalding is an author who, try as he might, can't seem to write anything serious. He's worked in the communications industry his entire life, mainly in media and marketing. As talking rubbish for a living can get tiresome (for anyone other than a politician), he thought he'd have a crack at writing comedy fiction - with an agreeable level of success so far, it has to be said. Nick lives in the South of England with his fiancée. He is approaching his forties with the kind of dread usually associated with a trip to the gallows, suffers from the occasional bout of insomnia, and still thinks Batman is cool.

Nick Spalding is one of the top ten bestselling authors in eBook format in 2012.

You can find out more about Nick by following him on Twitter or by reading his blog Spalding's Racket.

Printed in Great Britain
by Amazon